# GOK COOKS CHINESE

## GOK WAN

PHOTOGRAPHY BY JEMMA WATTS

MICHAEL JOSEPH *AN IMPRINT OF* PENGUIN BOOKS

MICHAEL JOSEPH

**Published by the Penguin Group**

**Penguin Books Ltd,** 80 Strand, London WC2R 0RL, England

**Penguin Group (USA) Inc.,** 375 Hudson Street, New York,
New York 10014, USA

**Penguin Group (Canada),** 90 Eglinton Avenue East, Suite 700,
Toronto, Ontario, Canada M4P 2Y3 (a division of Pearson Penguin Canada Inc.)

**Penguin Ireland,** 25 St Stephen's Green, Dublin 2, Ireland
(a division of Penguin Books Ltd)

**Penguin Group (Australia),** 250 Camberwell Road,
Camberwell, Victoria 3124, Australia (a division of Pearson Australia Group Pty Ltd)

**Penguin Books India Pvt Ltd,** 11 Community Centre, Panchsheel Park, New Delhi – 110 017, India

**Penguin Group (NZ),** 67 Apollo Drive, Rosedale, Auckland 0632, New Zealand (a division of Pearson New Zealand Ltd)

**Penguin Books (South Africa) (Pty) Ltd,** Block D, Rosebank Office Park, 181 Jan Smuts Avenue, Parktown North,
Gauteng 2193, South Africa

**Penguin Books Ltd,** Registered Offices: 80 Strand, London WC2R 0RL, England

www.penguin.com

First published 2012
1

Text copyright © Gok Wan, 2012

Programme, programme material and format copyright © Optomen Television Ltd, 2012

Photography copyright © Jemma Watts, 2012
except on pages 40, 63 and 239 copyright © Elise Dumontet, 2012

The moral right of the author has been asserted

Set in Mr and Mrs Eaves

Printed and bound by Firmengruppe APPL, aprinta druck, Wemding, Germany
Colour reproduction by Altaimage Ltd

A CIP catalogue record for this book is available from the British Library

ISBN: 978–0–718–15951–1

ALWAYS LEARNING        **PEARSON**

FOR MY WONDERFUL FAMILY
WHO HAVE FED ME THE MOST DELICIOUS FOOD
AND UNDYING LOVE FOR THE WHOLE OF MY LIFE.
THANK YOU. X

# MENU 菜单

# INTRODUCTION

'When I was younger, slaving over a wok in Dad's Chinese takeaway, I never imagined that one day I would be writing a cookbook full of my father's recipes. Arguing with him in the busiest of kitchens, I never imagined that I would one day thank him for his patience and guidance; that one day I would have the confidence to teach others – to share with you the secrets of my family's kitchen, taught to me by the greatest chef I know, Poppa Wan. I never imagined that you would want to listen . . .

Nowadays, it seems like everyone has eaten Chinese food and thinks they know what it's about: unhealthy, usually deep-fried and covered in pink and gloopy sweet and sour sauce. But I'm here to tell you that the Chinese food we're used to in the UK is a Western invention. The dishes my dad taught me to cook were quick and healthy, and very different to the sort of thing that most people have come to expect from their takeaways. My aim with this book is to show you all how easy, simple and tasty home-cooked Chinese food can be. I'm going to take out all the rubbish and leave all the good stuff in.

Food has been at the centre of my life ever since I can remember. Whether cooking for our loyal customers in the family restaurant or cooking to feed ourselves, food is a way of life for the Family Wan. Dad taught us that food wasn't just nutrition. He lives by one mantra and one mantra alone: 'We do not eat to live. We live to eat. We live for food.' It's a mantra that I now live my life by.

Food is important to Chinese culture – and when I say that, it's a total understatement! Everything in my father's culture revolves around food . . . happiness, sadness, forgiveness, even people's nicknames: I have a cousin we call 'Sweet Potato' and my best friend goes by the name of 'Chicken Leg'! I always say that a Chink without food is like a shoe without a heel: completely pointless. Food is just who we are. A lot of our conversations revolve around it – food is in our stories, colours our memories and is often used as analogies. One of my favourite memories is of my dad watching a football match on the edge of his seat. Michael Owen was running down the pitch to score a goal and suddenly Dad shouted at the television, 'Michael Owen, he got leg like chilli – hot and spicy!'

When I was growing up, Poppa Wan taught me about Hong Kong, his motherland. As a child he fed me stories of how he would cook potatoes in makeshift ovens made of rocks and wire, hidden in the mountains that surrounded his village. A man of few words, he is more skilled in the kitchen than the most practised magician. He has the natural ability to wow an audience into submission with one toss of his wok or a slice of his cleaver. He taught me to respect eating food, to enjoy the sharing of food with the people I care about most; he taught me that this is the secret behind Chinese cookery. It allows you a brand-new sense. Chinese cooking brings with it the sense of emotion. I never realized it as a child but every time my dad stir-fried, boiled, diced, sliced or steamed, he was teaching me a secret language – one filled with tradition, a sense of my heritage and also a bitter-sweet bereavement for a world he loves and misses.

One of the best heirlooms I have been given is a bunch of secret recipes passed down to me from my family. None contain magical ingredients and, in fact, most are simple and non-pretentious. I promise you, hand on wok, I will teach you everything I know with these dishes from the most amazing continent of flavour, Asia. Dishes my father taught me to cook and also dishes that I've found, whilst travelling in China, Hong Kong or Singapore, which I've tried to teach my father about. When I pick up a wok or a ladle it does something to me – in a weird way it almost completes me. It reminds me of where I'm from and who I want to be – someone who has been taught the skill of cooking and serving food, a skill which I owe to my father. Over the years, I've taken his recipes and developed them into a language of my own.

Nothing fills me with more happiness than looking after people. Whether I'm on set, dressing people and trying to understand how they feel about their bodies, or whether I'm at home, dressing my dinner table, about to cook a feast for my friends, it's all about love and connecting with people. Chinese food is the perfect vehicle to tell somebody you love them. It's not tough to make, but it is all about preparation, which allows you to execute a dish in seconds once you start to cook. It's this preparation that gives you the time to think about the person that you're cooking for – respecting what they already know but also taking them by the hand and leading them on a culinary journey to places that they might never have been before. I hope you enjoy the journey I'm going to take you on!

# ALL ABOUT INGREDIENTS

## THE THREE DEGREES

Whether you're knocking up a quick stir-fry or slowly braising meat you will, at some point, find yourself reaching for garlic, ginger and spring onions. As synonymous with Chinese cookery as garlic and onions are with French cuisine, these three stalwarts create a base on to which you can add a continent's worth of influences and flavours. I'd say these are the three most important ingredients in Chinese cookery. I like to refer to them as my 'Three Degrees': individually strong, but so much better when working in harmony with one another. Throughout this book you will find them sliced, diced, bashed and smashed Poppa Wan-styleee! The preparation method is specific to each dish and the part you want your Three Degrees to play, so follow the instructions carefully.

**GARLIC:** I love the taste of garlic – it has the most remarkable flavour. I use it in almost everything I cook. There's something about it which makes you feel less guilty about other, less healthy things you might be putting in your body. Clinically proven by scientists to be good for you, just make sure your date eats it too to avoid any embarrassing breath issues!

**GINGER:** Root ginger is an essential staple of Chinese cookery: not only does its unique flavour add warmth to dishes, but it also enhances the natural flavours of other ingredients, especially meats such as beef and pork. My mum doesn't really like ginger, so my dad makes sure he cuts it into large chunks so she can easily pick them out and put them to one side – that's love! It's crucial to have ginger in some dishes, so don't ever just leave it out. Buy it fresh in large hands and just snap off what you need – keeping a fresh supply means it's never woody inside and the skin is young so there's no need to peel it before chopping or slicing.

**SPRING ONIONS:** Two-tone in appearance, and two-tone in flavour and usage, the white part provides you with a distinctive onion taste, very often used at the beginning of a dish to add depth. The green stalks have a more subtle flavour, but bring vibrant colour to a dish, so are best for garnishing whilst still adding a light onion flavour. To prepare them, all you need is a damp cloth – gently wipe the length of the spring onion to clean it, and the top layer of skin will be taken off as well, which saves you having to peel it.

# MY CHINESE LOVE BASKET OF TASTE AND FLAVOUR

In my kitchen I keep a constantly stocked basket of bottled Chinese flavours. When I come to make something, all I need do is reach for my comfort blanket of condiments, and whatever I create will deliver the satisfying pang of the Orient I so often crave. In my basket I keep what I believe to be the essentials of Chinese cookery: bottles of fish sauce, light and dark soy sauce, Shaoxing rice wine, sesame oil, oyster sauce, rice wine vinegar and groundnut oil. These all have their place and represent the flavour building blocks you'll need when cooking Chinese food: fire, depth, warmth, spice – beautiful Asian flavours. I suggest you create your own love basket. All ingredients are available from your local supermarket, so there are no excuses. The Shaoxing rice wine can be substituted with dry sherry, but I urge you to pick up the real thing – you'll taste the difference in the finished dish.

**FISH SAUCE:** An absolute essential for Chinese cooking which tastes amazing. Use instead of salt to add a unique savoury flavour. A little goes a long way though – go easy. Remember, you can always add more but you can't take away.

**GROUNDNUT OIL:** The Italians use olive oil in their recipes, and the English like rapeseed oil to cook with, but the Chinese love groundnut oil. Originally used because it was cheap and easy to make, its light nuttiness has now become an indispensable taste in Chinese cookery. It is perfect for wok-frying as it has a high smoking point, meaning the oil won't burn and discolour your food at the fierce temperatures needed to get the best results.

**OYSTER SAUCE:** Don't be put off by thoughts of sucking down raw shellfish! Most oyster sauce contains just a small amount of oyster extract that gives it a unique taste. Deeply dark and rich, this provides a luxurious note to any dish it's added to and is often used in vegetable dishes to pump up the flavour.

**RICE VINEGAR:** Less harsh than its Western counterparts such as white wine vinegar or malt vinegar, this has a slight hint of sweetness that helps when balancing dishes. Many Sichuan dishes use rice vinegar to create the sweet and sour taste we know and love

in the UK. Once you try it you'll be converted and will think nothing of pouring it all over your chips!

**SESAME OIL:** This is not to be used for cooking with, but as a flavouring for dressing dishes just before serving. It has a beautifully mature smoky flavour, created by the gentle toasting of tiny sesame seeds. Totally unique and totally delicious.

**SHAOXING RICE WINE:** Tasting a little like granny's sherry, this ingredient, when added to food, will give your dishes a genuine Chinese flavour that you will no doubt recognize but could never replicate without this magic ingredient. Perfumed and complex, like any wine should be, it has a real Asian flavour (and smells a little like brandy or sherry that has gone off!).

**SOY SAUCE:** This condiment comes in both light and dark varieties, and is the most well-known flavouring of Chinese food. Light soy sauce is used most in cooking to add flavour, whereas dark soy sauce has a more subtle taste but helps to add a glossy darkness to finished dishes. Both are the product of a laborious fermentation process that allows the uniquely rich taste to develop. All that hard work comes to you in a bottle ready to pour, so take advantage and use liberally.

# CHINESE COOKERY ESSENTIALS

**BEANCURD (TOFU):** A soft, yielding, white and wobbly delight, beancurd, or tofu, is an Asian classic ingredient. It's very versatile, as it happily absorbs stronger flavours and spices, so is a great protein to use to pep up almost any vegetarian dish and seems to have a natural affinity with black bean sauce. I like to buy a big block of firm tofu and keep it covered in water in the fridge, slicing off what I need and chucking it in the wok.

**BEANSPROUTS:** These are the germinated sprouts of the mung bean, and have a wonderful delicate flavour and a moreish crunch. Use them as a vegetable accompaniment and to add texture to your salads, noodle dishes or spring rolls.

**CHILLI:** I love chilli. I've been raised on a diet of strong flavours so was used to its warmth and spicy kick from an early age. With chillies, the seeds add extra heat, so de-seed your chillies if you don't like lots of fire. To do it safely, cut in half lengthways and then flatten the whole chilli on your chopping board first to give you a steadier surface to work on, especially when using a cleaver. Turn your halved chilli over so the waxy skin is underneath and you won't slip when chopping.

**CHILLI BEAN PASTE:** This is a fiery Sichuan paste made from fermented broad beans, soy beans and chillies. It is so utterly moreish that you will soon be spreading it on your toast, but it is fierce, so add it in small amounts whilst you build up your resilience to the heat. It's hard to recommend a straightforward substitute here as it packs such a unique punch, but if you must go with a supermarket substitute then I recommend adding loads of chopped chilli to Japanese miso paste, which is now widely available.

**CHINESE CHILLI OIL:** I use a jarred variety of Chinese chilli oil that has huge lumps of chilli floating about in the bottom; I either spoon off just the oil to drizzle over a dish to dress it, or I really dig into the fiery bowels of the jar to reach the chilli in the base. You can buy chilli oil in most regular supermarkets these days, but my top tip is to add an extra kick by finely chopping red chillies and adding them to the bottle. This will infuse the oil, which will become hotter and hotter as time passes.

**CHINESE FRIED FISH BALLS:** These are commonly available in the chilled section of a Chinese supermarket. I am not going to pretend that they are good for you – they're made from cuttlefish and fried in huge vats of oil – but they taste AMAZING. Ready packed for your convenience they are a true taste of Hong Kong. Enjoy as a treat, but just make sure you add five minutes extra on to your gym visit in the morning!

**CHINESE LETTUCE:** Chinese lettuce is a pretty little lettuce complete with frilly trim. Don't get hung up on sourcing this ingredient as most other lettuces with some structure and body will suffice. Try Cos, Batavia, or baby gem lettuce as perfectly good substitutes.

**CHINESE SAUSAGE (LAP CHONG):** A simply divine ingredient with a distinct taste of the Orient. Made from an unlikely duo of pork meat and duck liver, this sausage is loaded with flavour. Chorizo would be the natural substitute to suggest, but the Spanish cured sausage has such a wonderful and particularly piquant character that it's actually quite different. In truth, there isn't a natural substitute for lap chong, so if you can't get your hands on it when you fancy trying that particular recipe, just add it to your shopping list for next time, turn over the page and try something else!

新竹米粉
BIHON
虎牌
您30多年的老朋友
創立於1970年
ISO22000
&
HACCP
NET WT : 8.92
虎牌正通實業股份有限公司
TIGER BRAND
INDUSTRIAL CO.,LTD

**CHINESE SESAME PASTE:** As the name suggests, this paste is made up of thousands of toasted sesame seeds that have been crushed and blitzed. Deliciously rich, it adds a touch of luxury to everything it comes into contact with – it's the Midas of Chinese ingredients. You can pick up tahini, the Mediterranean sesame paste, in most supermarkets, but as the sesame seeds in tahini are not toasted before crushing it is somehow not as tasty. If you are really stuck, then add a couple of teaspoons of sesame oil to a large dollop of peanut butter.

**CHINKIANG BLACK RICE VINEGAR:** Like all Asian vinegars, black rice vinegar is not as strong as its Western counterparts. Black rice vinegar carries a certain subtle sweetness which leads to a less harsh vinegar kick. If you can't get hold of the black vinegar then purchase the white version, commonly labelled as 'rice vinegar' and widely available from supermarkets (see page 17); there is very little difference in flavour, although appearance of the final dish will obviously change dramatically.

**CHOI SUM:** A mainstay vegetable of Chinese cuisine, the stalk provides a satisfying bite whilst its tender leaves are adept at mopping up excess sauce. If you can't find choi sum then opt for tenderstem broccoli or mature spinach.

**CORNFLOUR:** A fantastic natural thickener for sauces and stocks, which will never go lumpy. Mix up a small amount with a little cold water and add a little at a time to prevent your sauce congealing. I use my finger to mix it up, then 'pinch' it together before dribbling it in.

**DRESSINGS:** You can make all sorts of simple dressings with the basic condiments in my Chinese Love Basket of Taste and Flavour (see page 17) but my favourite is to make a simple soy sauce and honey dressing in a jam jar, which is good with so many things, and can also be used as a glaze or a dipping sauce. It's just normal runny honey mixed with soy sauce and whisked together. The saltiness of the soy and the sweetness of the honey are exactly what Chinese food is all about – yin and yang, sweet and savoury. To die for!

**DRIED LOTUS SEEDS:** These can be bought from Chinese supermarkets and must be soaked overnight before use to soften the tough outer skin before being added to soups, congee and other traditional dishes. The paste made from lotus seeds has a distinctive taste and is used in Asian desserts and pastries.

**DRIED RED DATES (JUJUBE FRUIT):** In health terms, the question here is 'What ailment does the red date not cure?' Widely acclaimed all over Asia as a medicinal, as well as a culinary, ingredient, the jujube fruit has a uniquely aromatic flavour. Used properly, it can form a crucial part of the flavour base for delicious broths (like Dad's Drunken Chicken, page 202). You can pick it up from one of those Chinese herbal shops that seem to be cropping up in almost every town centre from Billericay to Berwick. There is no direct substitute.

**DRIED SHRIMP:** These are delicious tiny nuggets of intense flavour. Use them in their original dried form to add a salty crunch to a recipe, or soak and then crush them into a paste to be stirred through almost any dish. It is seeking out and using this sort of ingredient that will take your version of Chinese cooking from the high street to the catwalk. Try soaked salt fish or jarred anchovy fillets as a substitute – but remember, you will never scale the heights of cooking haute couture if you don't have the right accessories.

**FERMENTED BLACK BEANS:** The unique and ubiquitous black bean of Chinese cookery is actually a soy bean that has been left to ferment. Like all fermented ingredients, these take on a mature flavour that is unique to itself and the process. Black beans become intensely salty and develop a flavour similar to that of soy sauce. Black beans are now synonymous with the Chinese takeaway, used to flavour endless foil trays of gloop; however, used properly, as they are in the recipes that follow, they complement other ingredients with their perfumed taste.

**FISH SAUCE:** See page 17.

**GARLIC:** See page 15.

**GINGER:** See page 15.

**GROUNDNUT OIL:** See page 17.

**GYOZA DUMPLING WRAPPERS:** These can be made very simply from flour and water. They are stronger than wonton skins, which are egg-based, and suit the cooking method for the 'potsticker' recipes in this book, as they have to withstand frying at a high temperature before being steamed.

**HO FUN NOODLES:** The Chinese equivalent to the Italian's pasta, noodles are the carbs of choice for Asian cuisine, second only to rice. There are many different types of noodles and each has a specific use in a dish, whether it's delicate strands of the glass-like vermicelli in a salad or the satisfying slurp of ho fun noodle in a soup.

**LAP CHONG:** See Chinese sausage, page 18.

**LOTUS LEAVES:** These are a beautiful ingredient: vibrant green with a vintage appearance, you will find these in their dried form in your local Chinese supermarket. Before use they need to be soaked in water for at least 40 minutes, which will make them malleable and easy to work with. If you can't get hold of them – they can be quite hard to find – then don't panic. You can generally substitute them with baking parchment although unfortunately you will then miss out on the beautifully subtle, almost tea-like, aroma that lotus leaves release during cooking.

**LOTUS ROOT:** Sold in tins, lotus root is a crunchy, sweet-tasting Asian root vegetable that grows in water. Like a long potato or squash on the outside, when sliced, it looks like delicate lace on the inside.

**MORNING GLORY:** This is a delicious vegetable very similar to choi sum in appearance and usage. First used in Chinese cooking for its medicinal purposes, it now stands out as an ingredient in its own right because of its delicious flavour. Named after the plant's propensity to unfurl its flowers in the morning it is well worth trying if you are looking in your local Chinese supermarket for something out of the ordinary. Do substitute tender-stem broccoli or mature spinach as an alternative.

**MUSHROOMS:** There are lots of different types of mushrooms used in Chinese cookery, but a couple of the most famous are probably straw mushrooms and shiitake mushrooms. Straw mushrooms are delicious: they grow under water and so can feel a bit slimy and spongy. They also look like eyeballs – it's hilarious to watch people try to eat them with chopsticks! Shiitake mushrooms are usually sold dried, so you need to soak them before use, and are great for adding an earthy flavour to broths and soups. Some other varieties of mushroom to look out for are elephant ear and enoki, or fall back on the old staple of the chestnut mushroom, widely available in most supermarkets.

**NUTS:** Used a lot in Chinese cuisine, particularly peanuts and cashews, nuts provide texture as well as flavour to dishes. The healthy option is to use raw or boiled nuts as these are less processed and have a pale, delicate colour that I love. Don't ever be tempted to use nuts that have been deep-fried and covered in salt, as this will ruin the finished dish.

**OYSTER SAUCE:** see page 17.

**PAK CHOI:** The most commonly recognized and widely available of the traditional Chinese vegetables, you will find pak choi in almost all large supermarkets. It is a deliciously subtle ingredient, full of texture, that bursts with flavour when bitten into. If you've tried this vegetable before and been underwhelmed, you must have been cooking it wrong! It is well worth reacquainting yourself, so simply steam whole and drizzle with a little light soy sauce, or follow the recipe for Choi Sum in Oyster Sauce on page 138.

**PRESERVED MUSTARD GREENS:** Mustard greens were originally brined to increase their longevity but have now become a real taste of the Orient in their own right. They add a sour punch to dishes they are added to. Try the Congee recipe on page 80 and add roughly chopped preserved mustard greens for a traditional take on a dish that is eaten by thousands throughout China for breakfast. At a push you could thoroughly rinse a gherkin of its vinegar and chop it into small pieces: it may lack the correct flavour but will, at least, give you the same texture.

**RED BEANCURD (GUI GEE):** Often referred to as 'Chinese cheese', don't be fooled into thinking this will be anything like your average Cheddar – the name is a false friend. Fermented tofu, pickled and traditionally dyed red to form an enticing and rich fleece, it is as unusual in appearance as it is in flavour. Nothing in the Western world compares to it, so it has no substitutes. The taste is what the Japanese refer to as 'umami' in its purest form.

**RICE STICK NOODLES:** Originally a product of Thailand, these noodles have become a staple in my cupboard. Soaked in hot water for a few minutes they begin to look not dissimilar to ho fun noodles. A perfect vehicle for almost any flavour, use them hot in stir-fries and soups or alternatively, once cooked, cool them and add to a salad to instantly transform it into a satisfying meal.

**RICE:** The ultimate Chinese carbohydrate, this is the Asian equivalent of the potato. Used to accompany almost every dish. The basic type of rice, suitable for almost all dishes in this book, is a long-grain rice.

**RICE VINEGAR:** See page 17.

**SESAME OIL:** See page 17.

**SHAOXING RICE WINE:** See page 17.

**SHRIMP PASTE:** A common ingredient all over Asia, shrimp paste is made by fermenting thousands of very tiny shrimps on huge open-air slabs. It has a very distinct, salty taste. Think of it as a Chinese version of tinned anchovies: just as the Italians would season a leg of lamb by studding it with slivers of anchovy, the Chinese use shrimp paste as part of a marinade to impart flavour. As they are so similar in taste, jarred anchovies are a good substitute.

**SOY SAUCE:** See page 15.

**SPRING ONIONS:** See page 17.

**SPRING ROLL WRAPPERS:** The outer casing of the familiar takeaway spring roll, these wrappers are formed from a very basic mixture of flour and water before being lightly fried. Making them correctly takes many generations' worth of skill, which is why it is so handy that you can now find ready-made versions in Chinese supermarkets and also a lot of health food stores. These dry out very quickly, so it's worth having a damp tea towel on hand to cover the packet as you make spring rolls.

**SICHUAN PEPPERCORNS:** If ever one ingredient could represent an entire cuisine, it would be the Sichuan peppercorn. So complex in flavour, with acidic, floral and spicy notes, they are not to everyone's palette, but if you like them, you generally become addicted and find a burning desire deep within to add them to almost everything you make! The cookery of the Southern Chinese province of Sichuan is all about the flavour profile of these peppercorns, and they provide a warmth and depth (and a numbness to your tongue!) to every dish they feature in. Their taste can't be replicated, so seek them out.

**VERMICELLI NOODLES:** Also known as glass noodles for their translucent appearance, these delicate, super-thin noodles are sold dried so must be rehydrated with hot water before being eaten. Like other types of noodle they are found all over the Asian continent, featuring in dishes from Hong Kong to Hanoi, and are a perfect base to accessorize with other flavours.

**VIETNAMESE RICE WRAPPERS:** As evident from their name, these translucent wrappers originated in Vietnam. They are dried before being sold and must be rehydrated in warm water before use. Dip them gently, one at a time, as they become incredibly fragile as soon as they are wet. Unlike Chinese spring roll wrappers these do not need to be cooked once they are rolled, and are usually used as the wrapper for a 'summer' roll (see page 166).

**WATER CHESTNUTS:** There is something truly magnificent about slicing through a water chestnut. The sound is spectacular and their crunchy texture is important in all Asian food. Not actually a nut at all, but an aquatic vegetable, they are available, tinned, in every supermarket.

**WHITE PEPPER:** I prefer to use white rather than black pepper so that you don't see black specks in the final dish. If you want a subtle spice hit, it's lighter than chilli and more forgiving.

**WONTON NOODLES:** Have two packets of fresh egg wonton noodles in the freezer and you will never go hungry! Treat them like delicate angel hair, and for the best results don't just use old packs that have been sitting in the cupboard, although dried egg noodles can be useful in a pinch. It's best to separate the individual strands out before putting them into a pan of boiling water. Once in, keep the noodles moving round so they don't stick together. The secret is to shock them in the boiling water, then rinse under the cold tap (to stop the cooking process), then add them back into the hot water briefly before putting them in a bowl and drizzling with sesame oil. Simple bliss! You will never have overcooked, mushy noodles again.

**WONTON WRAPPERS OR 'SKINS':** These wrappers are sheets of really thin pastry, as delicate as tissue paper, made out of wheat flour. Super-convenient to use and beautiful to look at when steamed, you can buy them from Chinese supermarkets and also online. They freeze really well but because they are delicate don't defrost them in the microwave – just leave them out on the side to thaw before using and don't handle them too much.

# ESSENTIAL EQUIPMENT

The beauty of cooking Chinese food is that you don't need a huge amount of specialist equipment to get fabulous results. At its most basic, you can achieve everything in this book with just a wooden chopping board, a wok, a cleaver and a ladle. Grab some bowls for preparing ingredients (and a bamboo steamer, too, if you want to be authentic), and you're away!

## WOODEN CHOPPING BOARD

Traditionally, Chinese cooks use circular wooden chopping boards to prepare all their food. If you're using wooden chopping boards, be aware that sometimes small splinters of wood can come away when you're chopping enthusiastically with your cleaver, especially on older boards. Take care of them by oiling them regularly and you'll prevent this happening. As well as chopping and slicing, try mixing elements like your dumpling fillings on a board instead of in a bowl – I do this in homage to my dad. And while you're doing it, have a little dance around your board – get physical with your food!

## WOK

THE piece of kit! Essentially just a deep-sided Chinese frying pan, get used to using a wok and I promise you it will become your best friend. There are two parts to a wok – the base and the ring around the sides. When cooking, all the heat goes to the centre of the wok and is transferred up and around the sides. The cooking happens at the bottom of the wok; once cooked you can push food to the sides if you want to keep it warm. Don't be scared of the heat – remember that you are in control of the cooking, so if the wok gets too hot, simply move it off the heat. The best thing about cooking with a wok is bare-minimum washing up (which personally I think is great, because I really hate washing up!).

## CLEAVER

Along with the wok, this is the most important bit of kitchen kit that you'll need for Chinese cooking. Sometimes called a 'chopper', you can do all sorts of jobs with it, including de-veining (or de-pooing!) prawns by scoring and scraping.

The base is good for fine chopping, as you can use your weight to control the blade, the middle is used for scoring meat or fish and the tip for slicing. Hundreds of years ago, monks in the mountains would have used them in exactly the same way as we do today. I've got so used to using a cleaver that I find it quite difficult to use Western knives now. All I can say is, get yourself a cleaver. They're quite cheap and will change the way you cook for good.

## LADLE

Cooking with a ladle can look a bit monstrous and bizarre, but this bad boy is key. It can scrape, scoop and pour – it can even be used to clean out your wok. You don't need anything fancy, just a basic metal ladle. Which just goes to show that rural cooking methods and utensils are the business – no fancy kitchen gadgets or gizmos are needed. It's how things have been done in Chinese kitchens for thousands of years.

## BOWLS AND BAMBOO STEAMERS

In my dad's restaurant we would cook with lots of bowls lined up in front of us holding the prepped ingredients. It's a great habit to get into – read the recipe all the way through, and then put each element into a separate bowl. Line them up on the counter ready for when you start cooking. Then you can be sure you've got everything you need, easily accessible. You won't get into a pickle and you'll be totally in control. Bamboo steamers are the traditional woven baskets that stack into towers for perfect dim sum and steamed meats and fish. But you don't need to use one: you can substitute a stainless-steel steamer basket, or just use your wok with a tight-fitting lid to create the same effect.

'THE PERFECT MEAL MUST ALWAYS BALANCE'

# 1

# CHINESE TAKEAWAY CLASSICS

Chinese takeaway food is something that everyone is familiar with and you've probably all got your absolute favourite dishes that you go back to every time. The thing about it is that the dishes have become Westernized over the years, full of gloopy sauces and, quite often, flavour enhancers like MSG, which are so not good for you. I'd like to use this chapter to show you how some of the more popular takeaway classics can taste when cooked at home. I hope you find one of your favourites in here.

**SERVES 4**

groundnut oil

2 Chinese sausages
(see page 18), thinly sliced
on the diagonal

2–3 eggs

salt and ground white pepper

300g long-grain rice,
cooked and chilled

75g frozen peas

7 water chestnuts, sliced

1 tin of anchovy fillets in oil,
drained and roughly chopped
into very small pieces

½–1½ tablespoons light
soy sauce, to taste

2 spring onions,
trimmed and sliced

**To serve**

Chinese chilli oil
(see page 18)

½ a round lettuce,
leaves separated

There are not enough words in the English dictionary to describe how much I love this dish. It just screams home comfort and I love the fact that you can eat this on its own and feel 100 per cent satisfied. You can literally add whatever you want: fish, meat, veg . . . it doesn't matter as it will all taste great. Think of it as a Chinese bubble and squeak – whatever you have in your fridge, lob it in! There are just a couple of rules to making fried rice that will guarantee a fabulous result. 1) Use day-old rice that has been cooled in the fridge. The reason for this is simple: rice that has sat overnight in the fridge will have dried out, whereas if you use hot, freshly cooked rice it will turn sticky and need a lot of oil to cook. 2) Don't use too much oil. This dish has been given a bad reputation over the years because of the word 'fried' in its title. But it's not deep-fried like chips. You only use as much oil as you would need to stir-fry the healthiest vegetable dish. That's it . . . so simple. Viva La Rice!

1. Heat a wok until medium hot and add a dash of oil. Add the Chinese sausage slices and fry quickly on both sides until coloured all over, with the white parts turning pink. Remove and set aside. Beat the eggs in a bowl and season with salt and pepper.

2. Add 1 tablespoon of oil to the hot wok and pour in the beaten eggs. Scramble the eggs, scraping the bits that are sticking to the wok. Aim for well-cooked scrambled egg that is separating into individual pieces. Once cooked, add the rice, scraping the bottom of the pan and tossing the rice as you heat it through. Once the rice is hot, add the remaining ingredients, except for the sausage. Continue to cook over a medium heat, tossing and mixing. Once the anchovies are beginning to melt into the hot rice, taste and season with pepper and a pinch of salt. Continue to stir-fry for 3–4 minutes, then taste and adjust the seasoning, adding more soy sauce if necessary.

3. Serve the fried rice with the cooked Chinese sausage, chilli oil and lettuce, wrapping spoonfuls of the rice inside the lettuce leaves to eat.

PREPARATION TIME 5 MINUTES     COOKING TIME 10 MINUTES

# 01. MY PERFECT FRIED RICE

## 02. SPICY STIR-FRIED PRAWNS WITH CASHEW NUTS

**SERVES 2**

**For the stock**

a 4cm piece of fresh ginger, cut in half and roughly bruised

2–3 cloves of garlic, peeled and roughly bruised

shells and heads from 8 raw king prawns (prawns used below)

**For the stir-fry**

2 tablespoons groundnut oil

a 2cm piece of fresh ginger, peeled and thinly sliced

2 cloves of garlic, peeled and roughly chopped

4 spring onions, trimmed, green and white parts separated, whites roughly bruised

8 raw king prawns, peeled and de-veined

3 sticks of celery, trimmed and thinly sliced on the diagonal

1 long red chilli, deseeded and finely chopped

salt and ground white pepper

1–2 teaspoons Shaoxing rice wine or dry sherry

2 teaspoons light soy sauce

1–2 teaspoons fish sauce, to taste

a pinch of sugar

100g cashew nuts

1 heaped teaspoon cornflour mixed with a little cold water

1 teaspoon sesame oil

There is so little wastage when cooking Chinese food – if making a king prawn dish like this one, all the shells and prawn heads can be used to make a delicious stock. When you've shelled the prawns – I always wear a pair of rubber gloves when I'm preparing this dish, as I can't stand the smell of prawns on my hands – pile the shells, tails and heads into a pan of boiling water, add some garlic and smashed ginger and you have a gorgeous and tasty stock. Use this stock to add flavour and balance to any dish, be it meat, fish or vegetables. This is how cooking should be – free! As Poppa Wan always says, 'No waste it . . . it add fravor, innit!'

1. For the stock, place the ginger, garlic and prawn shells and heads into a wok or saucepan. Cover with water and bring to the boil. Once boiling reduce the heat and gently simmer for up to 1 hour (although 10–15 minutes is fine). Drain the liquid through a sieve lined with muslin before using, discarding the spices, shells and heads.

2. Heat the oil in a wok over a high heat. Add the ginger, garlic and spring onions (both green and white parts) and cook for a minute or until the garlic has softened and the ginger is aromatic. Add the prawns and cook for a further minute, then add the celery and ¾ of the chilli.

3. Once the prawns start to turn pink, add 4 tablespoons of stock (the rest of the stock can be used in other recipes) and season with salt and pepper. Add the Shaoxing rice wine, soy sauce and fish sauce. Taste, and if the mixture is too salty, add a pinch of sugar. Add the cashews and dot in ½–1 teaspoon of the cornflour mix to slightly thicken the dish.

4. Serve the prawns sprinkled with the remaining chopped chilli and a drizzle of sesame oil. If you like, you can use a large savoy cabbage leaf as a bowl.

PREPARATION TIME 10 MINUTES
COOKING TIME 1 HOUR 10 MINUTES

4 tablespoons hoisin sauce

2 tablespoons yellow
bean sauce (optional)

1–2 cloves of garlic, peeled
and finely chopped

a 1cm piece of fresh ginger,
peeled and cut
into matchsticks

1 star anise

4 teaspoons caster sugar

¼ teaspoon Chinese
five-spice powder

2 tablespoons honey, plus a
little extra for drizzling

1 pork loin (approx. 700g)

Barbecuing is a popular cooking technique that Asia has taken total ownership of. You only have to stroll through Chinatown to see all the tempting barbecued meat and fish on display, draped on S-hooks in the windows of restaurants like beautiful gowns in designer boutiques. Marinated duck with its coat of glossy autumnal browns and caramels; pork belly with its crispy skin that looks like it's been dipped in precious stones; and elegant soy sauce chicken, proud like the finest cashmere. And finally, the haute couture of the barbecue-world, char siu pork; its marbled hues of red and orange served juxtaposed against simple white rice – Fashion Week eat your heart out!

1. Put all the ingredients apart from the pork loin into a bowl and mix together (or you can place the marinade in a plastic freezer bag and add the pork fillet). Smother the loin with the mixture and place in the fridge to marinate for a minimum of 2 hours, and preferably overnight.

2. When ready to cook the meat, preheat the oven to 210°C/410°F/ gas 6. Remove the pork from the fridge (best results are achieved if you leave it to warm to room temperature, but this is not essential). Place the marinated meat on a flat baking tray lined with foil. Spoon over as much of the remaining marinade as possible. Put the meat into the oven and roast for 10 minutes.

3. Reduce the oven temperature to 180°C/350°F/gas 4 and roast for a further 40–45 minutes, turning and basting the meat with the marinade as it cooks. Remove the meat from the oven once cooked through and glossy.

4. Carve the meat and serve drizzled with a little honey.

PREPARATION TIME 2 HOURS MINIMUM    COOKING TIME 50 MINUTES

# 03. POPPA WAN'S HONEY-GLAZED CHAR SIU PORK

**SERVES 3–4**

1 tablespoon groundnut oil

2 cloves of garlic, peeled and finely sliced

½ a fresh red chilli, deseeded and thinly sliced

a 3cm piece of fresh ginger, peeled and cut into matchsticks

4 spring onions, finely chopped

4 tinned water chestnuts, drained and thinly sliced

2 tablespoons skinless peanuts, boiled for 10 minutes

2 tablespoons dried shrimps (see page 20)

1 tablespoon Shaoxing rice wine or dry sherry

250g fine French beans, topped and tailed

2 teaspoons fish sauce

3 tablespoons light soy sauce

a pinch of caster sugar

ground white pepper

2 teaspoons sesame oil

I firmly believe there is no such thing as a hungry Chinese vegetarian. I spent years not eating meat and I used to get sick of going for Italian, French or English food and not being able to eat anything other than a stuffed pepper. Chinese cuisine respects vegetables 100 per cent, and often more thought goes into preparing a bowl of beans, a dish of aubergine or a plate of Chinese lettuce than the stewing of the main meat dish. These green beans are an amazing accompaniment or a dish to be enjoyed in its own right, full of goodness and vitamins designed to give you health, wealth and happiness after your meal.

1. Heat the oil in a wok over a high heat. Once hot, add the garlic and chilli and stir-fry for 10 seconds to soften. Add half the ginger and all the spring onions, along with the water chestnuts, peanuts and dried shrimps, and cook for 30 seconds.

2. Add the green beans to the wok and toss well. The beans should begin to blister and turn slightly golden. Once everything begins to soften, add the Shaoxing rice wine, fish sauce and soy sauce and cook for a further 10 seconds.

3. Add 4 tablespoons of hot water. Leave to steam for a further 4–5 minutes until the water is almost evaporated and the beans are hot through but still crunchy.

4. Add the remaining ginger and season the mixture with caster sugar, white pepper and sesame oil.

5. Serve piping hot.

PREPARATION TIME 15 MINUTES    COOKING TIME 7 MINUTES

# 04. AROMATIC WOK-FRIED BEANS

**SERVES 2**

1 small head of broccoli
(approx. 250g), cut
into small florets

3 teaspoons sesame oil

a pinch of salt

1 tablespoon groundnut oil

a 2cm piece of fresh ginger,
peeled and finely chopped

2 or 3 cloves of garlic,
peeled and thinly sliced

1 spring onion, finely
chopped (optional)

1 tablespoon fermented
black beans (see page 20),
soaked for 5 minutes in
warm water and drained

1 beef sirloin steak (approx.
250g), sliced into strips,
excess fat removed if desired

1 fresh red chilli, deseeded
and finely chopped

ground white pepper

1 tablespoon Shaoxing
rice wine or dry sherry

light soy sauce, to taste

### For the quick pickled chilli

1 fresh red chilli, sliced into
long diagonal strips

2 tablespoons rice vinegar

1–2 teaspoons caster sugar

Black bean sauce dishes are arguably the most famous on any Chinese takeaway menu. Salty, and often with a chilli kick, this familiar friend will deliver when your tastebuds crave the flavours of Asian food – but this recipe is a far healthier and more stripped-down version of the 'Number 42' classic most of you will recognize. I've replaced the traditional chunks of green pepper and onion with blanched broccoli, and thinned out the sauce to enable your senses to truly fall in love with the main attraction: the Mighty Black Bean.

1. To make the quick pickled chilli, put the strips of chilli into a bowl and cover with rice vinegar. Sprinkle with the caster sugar and leave to soak while you continue with the rest of the recipe.

2. Blanch the broccoli in salted boiling water for 2 minutes. Drain, then season with a drizzle of sesame oil and a pinch of salt. Mix well and set aside.

3. Heat a wok over a high heat and add a glug of oil. Add the ginger, garlic and spring onion and stir-fry for 10 seconds, or until the garlic is tender. Add the black beans and cook for 20 seconds, stirring and tossing.

4. Add the strips of steak and cook for 2–3 minutes, to seal on all sides. Add the chilli, blanched broccoli and a little pinch of salt and pepper, along with the Shaoxing rice wine, 1 teaspoon of soy sauce and 1 tablespoon of water. Toss to mix well. Taste and adjust the seasoning as necessary.

5. Drain the pickled chilli and serve on the side as an optional fiery kick to the beef and broccoli.

PREPARATION TIME 10 MINUTES
COOKING TIME 8 MINUTES

# 05. BEEF IN FRAGRANT BLACK BEAN SAUCE

**SERVES 2**

1 tablespoon groundnut oil

1 small onion, peeled and finely sliced

4 eggs

salt and ground white pepper

1 tablespoon light soy sauce

2 teaspoons fish sauce

4 tablespoons peas, fresh or frozen

150–200g freshly cooked, picked white crabmeat

2 spring onions, shredded

**To garnish**

a handful of pea shoots

Nothing says comfort like a home-cooked meal, and this dish is firmly cemented in the *Family Wan Comfort Cookbook*. Dad would usually serve this dish alongside steamed salt fish, squid and lap chong (the smoky-sweet sausage that's the Chinese equivalent of chorizo), as this simple Chinese omelette is perfect for balancing strong flavours. I've used crabmeat here as a tasty alternative to squid. We would usually eat this meal on a Sunday night as it's super quick to make and always tastes better eaten on your lap in front of the TV. I hope one day I will pass this treasured eating experience on to my own family and I am confident it will mean just as much to them as it does to me now.

1. Heat a wok over a medium heat and add a dash of oil. Add the sliced onion and cook, tossing and stirring over the heat, until softened and colouring at the edges.

2. Meanwhile beat the eggs in a bowl and season with a pinch of salt and pepper, ½ tablespoon of soy sauce and the fish sauce.

3. Add the peas to the wok along with 1 tablespoon of water, and stir until almost cooked through. If using frozen peas this will take a little longer than with fresh. Allow the water to evaporate from the wok.

4. Add the seasoned beaten egg to the wok, stirring it into the other ingredients. Cook the egg as if you were scrambling it, letting small clumps of egg form in the pan rather than a whole omelette. Taste and adjust the seasoning as necessary, adding a little more soy and/or fish sauce if needed.

5. Once the egg is almost cooked, add the crabmeat around the sides of the wok, sprinkling a little over the top of the egg. Warm the crabmeat through and add the spring onions. Fold everything together, then taste and adjust the seasoning if necessary.

6. Spoon the mixture on to a serving platter and garnish with the pea shoots.

PREPARATION TIME 10 MINUTES    COOKING TIME 10 MINUTES

# o6. CRABMEAT AND SWEET PEA FOO YUNG

**SERVES 2**

2 tablespoons potato flour, or cornflour

salt and ground white pepper

4 boneless and skinless chicken thighs, cut into bite-size pieces

groundnut oil, to shallow fry

4 cloves of garlic, peeled and sliced

3 spring onions, cut into batons

2 tablespoons Shaoxing rice wine or dry sherry

1–2 tablespoons soy sauce

a pinch of caster sugar

Roll up your sleeves, focus in on your opponents, concentrate and go . . . Finger food at the Chinese dinner table is a little like the clash of the Titans: the first one to the plate is guaranteed a mouthful of happiness, and there's no room for losers – no pain, no gain. Growing up as a child, my elder brother and I could take on the skill and speed of the Williams sisters when it came to a culinary tennis match. A plate of garlic chicken on the table can turn the most unlikely of athletes into gold medallists. Forget the chopsticks – get your hands in first and the prize is yours!

1. Put the potato flour into a shallow bowl and season generously with salt and pepper. Dust the chicken pieces in the flour, shaking off any excess, then set aside.

2. Heat a wok over a high heat and add the oil. Once hot, add the chicken pieces and shallow fry (in batches if necessary) for 3–4 minutes, or until golden and slightly crisp on the outside and cooked through in the middle. Remove from the wok with a slotted spoon and drain on kitchen paper, then set aside. Clean out the wok.

3. Add a dash of oil to the clean wok and heat over a medium to high heat. Add the garlic and spring onions and stir-fry for 1–2 minutes, or until the garlic is tender and aromatic. Add the Shaoxing rice wine, soy sauce, sugar and a pinch of pepper. Heat through and taste, adjusting the seasoning as necessary.

4. Put the chicken back into the pan and stir it into the sauce, mixing it well with the garlic and spring onions.

5. Taste, add a little more soy or seasoning if needed, and serve.

PREPARATION TIME 10 MINUTES    COOKING TIME 15 MINUTES

**SERVES 6–8**

2 x 170g tins of white
crabmeat in brine
or water, drained

1 x 425g tin of creamed corn

1 x 198g tin of sweetcorn

2 eggs, beaten

2 tablespoons light soy sauce

salt and ground white pepper

1 tablespoon cornflour,
mixed with 2 tablespoons
water

1–2 teaspoons sesame
oil, to taste

**To garnish**

2 spring onions,
finely chopped

One of my earliest food memories is of eating crab and sweet-corn soup. We would serve this beautiful thick broth to almost every customer in the restaurant and they loved it. Dad was the first restaurateur in Leicester to introduce dishes like this on to his menus. Until then, the only Chinese food readily available was a generic Chop Suey-style dish – gloopy gravy packed with Wai Ching (MSG) and not really very Chinese at all. In fact, if I recall correctly, most Chinese restaurant menus had more British dishes on them than Asian ones (for example, I'm not quite sure how you'd make a Chinese steak and chips!). Our more cultured palates may now consider this soup as common, but back then it was new, modern, exotic and fascinating ... My God, it was Asian!

1. Heat 1 litre of water in a wok or pan over a medium heat until gently simmering. Add the drained crab, creamed corn and sweetcorn, plus any juices in the tin. Stir well to mix, then cook at a gentle simmer for 5–10 minutes, to allow the flavours to mix.

2. Drop in the beaten eggs and swirl them around in the water so that the egg cooks in strands. Season with the soy sauce and a good pinch of pepper.

3. Stir in the cornflour paste, continuing to stir until the soup is thickened. Taste and adjust the seasoning as necessary, adding a little more soy sauce if needed.

4. Finish the soup with a couple of drops of sesame oil sprinkled on the top to taste. Spoon into serving bowls and garnish with the chopped spring onions.

PREPARATION TIME 5 MINUTES     COOKING TIME 15 MINUTES

# o8. SIMPLE CRAB AND SWEETCORN SOUP

**SERVES 2**

2 tablespoons potato flour,
or cornflour

salt and ground white pepper

2 beef sirloin steaks
(approx. 200g each),
trimmed of fat, sliced
into 0.5cm strips

6 tablespoons groundnut oil

a 4cm piece of fresh ginger,
peeled and finely chopped

2 cloves of garlic,
peeled and chopped

3 spring onions, chopped

I medium carrot, peeled and
cut into matchsticks

2 tablespoons light soy sauce

½–I teaspoon caster sugar

I teaspoon sesame oil

I–I½ teaspoons rice vinegar
or cider vinegar, to taste

**To garnish**

chilli flakes

Crispy fried shredded beef is a Chinese takeaway staple; everyone seems to have tried this dish and fallen in love with it . . . except me. Chinese food should be fresh and fragrant, and you should be able to taste every single layer of flavour that the chef has developed for you. The moment you start coating things in batter and deep frying, then adding gloopy sauces, the result you get is only a homogenized hint of what the real experience should have been. I've developed this NAKED version of crispy shredded beef for you, which I promise will allow every single flavour to jump around in your mouth like a taste circus. Hold on tight, the ride's about to begin . . .

1. Put the potato flour into a bowl and season generously with salt and pepper. Add the sliced beef and dust it in the flour, then remove the beef, shaking off any excess.

2. Heat the oil in a wok. When it's hot, add the beef and cook until just crisp on the outside, working in batches if necessary. Drain on kitchen paper and set to one side. Clean out the wok.

3. Add a dash of oil to the clean wok. Add the ginger, garlic, spring onions and carrot and fry over a high heat for 1 minute, or until aromatic. Add the soy sauce, sugar, sesame oil, vinegar and a pinch of pepper, along with 3 tablespoons of water to create a sauce. Heat until the sugar has dissolved. Taste and adjust the flavours, adding more sugar or vinegar as necessary.

4. Add the beef to the wok and gently mix into the sauce. Remove from the heat and garnish with chilli flakes. Serve with rice.

PREPARATION TIME 10 MINUTES    COOKING TIME 15 MINUTES

**SERVES 2**

2 tablespoons cornflour

3 tablespoons Shaoxing rice wine or dry sherry

4 tablespoons light soy sauce

2 chicken breasts, cut on an angle into 1cm-thick slices

4 tablespoons groundnut oil

2 large, dried chillies

2 teaspoons Sichuan peppercorns (optional), (see page 22)

2 cloves of garlic, peeled and finely sliced

3 spring onions, sliced into 2cm rounds

4 tablespoons water

2 tablespoons dark soy sauce

2 teaspoons toasted sesame oil

60g plain peanuts

2 tablespoons fresh coriander, roughly chopped

Chinese cookery is predominantly split between two styles of food that originate in different provinces: Canton and Sichuan. Cantonese-style cooking tends to be simple with subtle flavours, in contrast to the hot and spicy mountain-cuisine of Sichuan. This chicken dish is a classic of Sichuan as it boasts the properties of fire and wealth through deep layers of spice. When this dish is cooked in a Western kitchen, I often find it to be too hot, so I urge you to try this stripped-down version which still nods in respect to Sichuan province. Enough spice in your life to serve at your table.

1. Tip the cornflour into a bowl and pour in 1 tablespoon of the Shaoxing rice wine and 2 tablespoons of the light soy sauce. Add the chicken and mix well, then cover and refrigerate, leaving to stand for at least 20 minutes (or overnight for convenience).

2. Heat 2 tablespoons of groundnut oil in a wok over a medium to high heat. Once hot, drain the chicken from the marinade, add the chicken to the wok and stir-fry for 3–4 minutes. (It's not necessary for the chicken to be cooked through at this point as it will be cooked further later on.) Remove the chicken to a plate and leave to one side.

3. Wipe out your wok with kitchen paper and pour in the remaining groundnut oil. Again, heat the oil over a medium to high heat. Once hot, add the dry chillies and stir-fry for 1 minute before adding the peppercorns, garlic and spring onions. Continue to stir-fry for a further minute.

4. Tip the chicken back into the wok and stir-fry for another minute. Pour in the water, along with the remaining Shaoxing rice wine, light and dark soy sauce, then bring to the boil and simmer for 30 seconds.

5. Add the sesame oil and peanuts, then heat through for a further 30 seconds before sprinkling with coriander and serving with rice.

PREPARATION TIME 10 MINUTES    COOKING TIME 10 MINUTES

# 10. **SPICY SICHUAN CHICKEN**

4 tablespoons groundnut oil

600g raw king prawns,
peeled and de-veined

1 onion, peeled and
diced into chunky cubes

1 green pepper, deseeded and
diced into chunky cubes

3 cloves of garlic,
peeled and finely sliced

2 tablespoons Shaoxing
rice wine or dry sherry

50ml water

2 tablespoons light
soy sauce

2 tablespoons yellow
bean sauce

2 tablespoons cashew nuts

I like my food how I like my boys: filling, flirtatious and with more flavour than I know what to do with! In the Chinese kitchen there are three main flavours that I like to flirt with – let me introduce you to my boys. I love black bean because he's dangerous, hoi sin because he's sweet and yellow bean because he lets me take control. Yellow bean sauce is so selfless he'll allow you to add anything – be it prawns, beef, chicken or veg – and will complement it with his natural flavour. He's understated and shy, but when you need him his loyalty is undeniable.

1. Heat 2 tablespoons of the oil in a wok over a high heat. When hot, add the king prawns. Stir-fry for 2–3 minutes until the prawns have changed to a vibrant pink and almost cooked through. Remove the prawns to a plate and keep to one side for later.

2. Wipe the wok with a piece of kitchen roll, then pour in the remaining oil and heat. When hot, add the onion and green pepper. Stir-fry for 3 minutes so that the onion starts to colour and the green pepper begins to blister.

3. Add the garlic and continue to stir-fry for a further 2 minutes before adding the Shaoxing rice wine, water and soy sauce. Bring the mixture back to the boil and tip in the yellow bean sauce. Return to the boil and reduce to a simmer for 2 minutes.

4. Tip the prawns back into the mixture and warm through for a further 2 minutes, then add the nuts and combine.

5. Serve immediately with rice.

PREPARATION TIME 10 MINUTES    COOKING TIME 15 MINUTES

# 11. **PRAWNS IN YELLOW BEAN SAUCE**

**SERVES 4**

1.5 litres vegetable stock

50g field mushrooms, sliced reasonably thickly

I teaspoon dried chilli flakes

50ml light soy sauce

75g tinned bamboo shoots, drained

a 5cm piece of fresh ginger, peeled and roughly sliced

3 cloves of garlic, peeled and bruised

I tablespoon granulated sugar

4 tablespoons rice or cider vinegar, according to taste

2 eggs, beaten

I tablespoon chopped chives

Opposites attract! This statement has never been more true than when it is applied to Chinese food. The most glorious balance of yin and yang is found in most Asian dishes. Sweet and sour, the two tastes that demonstrate this balance perfectly, are at the heart of this dish. Sourness is perfectly harnessed in rice vinegar and light soy sauce, offset and complemented by the sweetness of field mushrooms and young ginger. Although simple to make, the audience at your dinner table will be wowed by how complex this soup tastes.

1. Pour the stock into a large saucepan and bring to the boil. Once it is boiling, reduce the heat to a simmer and add all the other ingredients apart from the vinegar, eggs and spring onions. Simmer the broth for 8–10 minutes so that the flavours combine.

2. Add the vinegar a little at a time. It is up to you how sour you enjoy your soup. Continue to simmer for a further 2 minutes.

3. Make sure the soup is simmering, not boiling, then gently whisk the soup while slowly pouring in the egg. The soup will turn cloudy before the strands of egg cook. Gently simmer the soup for 2 minutes once all the egg has been added.

4. Divide the soup between bowls and dress with the chopped chives.

PREPARATION TIME 5 MINUTES    COOKING TIME 25 MINUTES

# 12. **HOT AND SOUR SOUP**

500g medium egg noodles

1 tablespoon sesame oil

2 tablespoons groundnut oil

3 cloves of garlic, peeled
and finely sliced

300g fresh raw prawns,
peeled and de-veined

200g mangetout,
thoroughly washed

2 tablespoons Shaoxing
rice wine or dry sherry

2 tablespoons light soy sauce

2 tablespoons dark soy sauce

salt and ground white pepper

2 spring onions, finely
shredded into 4cm long strips

1 carrot, peeled and cut
into matchsticks

This recipe is the perfect example of how you can change a stodgy takeaway dish into a delicious, healthy and fresh dinner. Choose your ingredients well and cook them carefully. Good quality king prawns and fresh vegetables cooked quickly will keep all their flavour and goodness locked in. I like to use fresh egg noodles from the Chinese supermarket – their taste and texture is simply divine. However dried egg noodles cooked to the packet instructions are a worthy substitute.

1. Cook the noodles according to the packet instructions, then drain and tip into a bowl. Pour over the sesame oil, tossing thoroughly to coat the noodles. Put to one side.

2. Heat the groundnut oil in a wok over a high heat. Once hot, add the garlic and stir-fry for 30 seconds before adding the prawns. Continue to stir-fry for 2–3 minutes. The prawns should begin to turn pink and a little brown on some of the edges.

3. Add the mangetout and mix to incorporate. Pour in the Shaoxing rice wine and leave to almost evaporate before adding the cooked and reserved noodles. Toss so that all of the ingredients are well mixed.

4. Turn the heat down to medium and add both of the soy sauces and a pinch of salt and pepper. Stir-fry for a further 2 minutes before spooning on to a plate and dressing with the spring onions and carrots.

5. Serve immediately as a delicious dinner.

PREPARATION TIME 5 MINUTES    COOKING TIME 15 MINUTES

# 13. PRAWN CHOW MEIN

'FEED HUNGRY MOUTHS WITH TASTY JOY'

# 2

## CHINESE SUNDAY ROAST: DIM SUM

Dim sum is the perfect excuse for meeting up with friends to catch up on all the gossip, whilst eating delicious food. To the Chinese, this is their version of a Sunday roast or brunch and is a tradition that goes back thousands of years. When eating dim sum at a restaurant, expect to see the waiters constantly passing your table with trolleys stacked high with bamboo baskets of steamed buns, filled with surprises like char siu (barbecued) pork, or richly flavoured mushrooms, warming bowls of congee (Chinese porridge), steamed rice parcels and delicious little potsticker dumplings. These dishes are not hard to make, so here is a selection for you to try at home. All you need to decide now is who to invite round for a gossip!

**SERVES 4**

8–10 raw prawns, peeled, de-veined and roughly chopped

4–5 small scallops with roe attached, roughly chopped

3 tinned water chestnuts, drained and diced

salt and ground white pepper

½ teaspoon sesame oil

1 egg, separated

a bunch of fresh chives, half roughly chopped, half left whole

cornflour, to dust

16 small yellow egg wonton wrappers (see page 23)

1 tablespoon groundnut oil

**To serve**

light soy sauce

chilli oil

If, like me, you love entertaining but your work commitments mean you often don't even have time to pick up fish and chips in the evening then I urge you to make a little time to prepare these dumplings in advance so you don't miss out on the party! Dim sum is brilliant for the time-poor as it's really all about the organization and these little dumplings of love are the perfect example. Simply make, chill in the fridge and, when you need them, pile into steamers, cook and serve. Simple. Mine's a G&T!

1. Mix together the prawns, scallops and water chestnuts. Season with a pinch of salt and pepper and add the sesame oil. Beat the egg white until lightly frothy, then measure out 1 tablespoon. Add this to the bowl and discard the remainder of the egg white. Then add the chopped chives and combine, squeezing everything between your fingers until it's well mixed but still has a bit of texture.

2. Dust a work surface with cornflour and lay the wonton wrappers on top. Dust your hands with cornflour and pick up a wonton wrapper. Put 1–2 teaspoons of the prawn and scallop mixture in the centre of the wrapper and brush the edges with egg yolk. Bring the corners together over the middle of the mixture, then squeeze and twist the top to make a shape like a small sack. Tie a whole chive around the thinnest part, trimming off any excess. Repeat with the remaining mixture.

3. Brush a heatproof plate with the groundnut oil and place it in your bamboo steamer. Put the dumplings on the plate and add a drop of water to the top of each dumpling where the wonton wrapper is tied. Place the steamer over a wok or pan of boiling water and steam for 5–8 minutes until the dumplings are just cooked through.

4. Remove from the steamer and serve with a little soy sauce and chilli oil on the side as a dip. Eat immediately.

PREPARATION TIME 35 MINUTES    COOKING TIME 10 MINUTES

## 14. PRAWN AND SCALLOP MONEYBAG DUMPLINGS

2 medium squid (tubes
and tentacles), cleaned

2 spring onions,
finely chopped

2 tablespoons groundnut oil

½ a fresh red chilli,
finely chopped

3 cloves of garlic, peeled
and finely chopped

salt and ground white pepper

**For the cucumber salad**

½ a cucumber, deseeded and
sliced into thin ribbons

4 tablespoons rice vinegar

a pinch of caster sugar

Without fail, whenever my family and I eat out we will always order this dish. There is something just beautiful about the texture of squid that I love and it's a great alternative to meat. The seasoning of this dish – garlic, chilli and spring onions – is divine sprinkled on to fluffy white rice: salty and crunchy with a real spicy kick. Most restaurants cook the squid by coating it in a cornflour and egg batter, but to be health conscious I've developed this recipe without the deep-frying stage. I have to say, I think it tastes just as good. And by not battering and deep-frying the squid, it allows you more control over the cooking process, which is useful as you don't want to overcook the squid and let it get rubbery. Enjoy!

1. Place the cucumber on a serving plate. Pour over the vinegar and a pinch of sugar and leave to one side.

2. Slice the squid tubes in half lengthways and lay them on to your board so that the inside is facing you. Using a sharp knife carefully score the tubes at an angle about 5mm apart, taking care not to slice all the way through. Turn the squid 45 degrees and repeat the scoring process at that angle. Once scored, slice the squid into 2cm wide strips. Cut any large tentacles in half and leave small ones whole.

3. Heat the wok over a meduim to high heat and add the oil. Add the chilli, garlic and spring onions and fry with a good pinch of salt and pepper. Continue to fry for 4–5 minutes, or until the mixture begins to dry out, being careful not to burn the garlic. Once dried out, remove from the pan and drain on kitchen paper.

4. Place the wok back on the heat and, once hot, add a dash of oil. When the oil is smoking, add the squid and stir-fry for 1 minute, or until half cooked through and charred a little on the edges. Put the drained garlic/chilli/spring onion mix back into the pan and stir through, tossing over the heat until the squid is just cooked. Taste and adjust the seasoning.

5. Serve with the cucumber garnish alongside.

PREPARATION TIME 10 MINUTES    COOKING TIME 10 MINUTES

# 15. CHILLI AND SALT SQUID WITH CUCUMBER SALAD

# 16. POPPA WAN'S AMAZING PORK RIBS

**SERVES 4 AS DIM SUM**

700g pork ribs, cut into 3cm pieces (I use my trusty cleaver, but it's easiest to ask your butcher to do this)

2 tablespoons black beans

a 3cm piece of fresh ginger, peeled and cut into matchsticks

2 cloves of garlic, peeled and finely diced

2 spring onions, finely sliced into rounds

salt and ground white pepper

The Western view of Chinese food, formed from eating the 'traditional' takeaway, is that it's a cuisine that's normally deep-fried and unhealthy, smothered in gloopy sauces. Proper Chinese food isn't. It is light and healthy, full of flavour and you'll be left wanting more. Get in there! These steamed pork ribs are one of my dad's signature dishes. This method of cooking completely respects the ingredients, as there is no sauce to mask the flavours of the pork and the black beans and you'll feel entirely virtuous for steaming your food.

1. Place the pork rib pieces in a colander and run them under cold water for about 5 minutes, until the outsides begin to turn white, then pat dry carefully with kitchen paper.

2. Put the black beans into a bowl and cover them with lukewarm water. Soak for 3 minutes, then drain.

3. Put the pork into a bowl or plate that will fit into your steamer. Top with the black beans and remaining ingredients.

4. Place the bowl in your steamer and steam for 25–35 minutes. The meat should be meltingly tender and pulling away from the bone, so continue cooking until this point is reached.

5. Remove from the heat and serve immediately, spooning over the sauce at the bottom of the bowl. Enjoy with rice as part of a main meal, or simply on their own.

PREPARATION TIME 10 MINUTES    COOKING TIME 30–40 MINUTES

3 dried lotus leaves
(see page 21), soaked in water
for at least one hour

300g glutinous rice

350ml water

4 dried shiitake mushrooms,
soaked in warm water
for 10 minutes

3 fresh shiitake mushrooms,
sliced

2 tablespoons groundnut oil

3 cloves of garlic,
peeled and finely sliced

a 3cm piece of fresh ginger,
peeled and finely sliced

3 spring onions, finely sliced

50g skinless and unsalted
peanuts, roughly chopped

2 dried scallops, broken up
into little pieces, soaked in
warm water for 10 minutes
(optional)

2 tablespoons Shaoxing
rice wine or dry sherry

1 tablespoon light soy sauce

2 tablespoons fish sauce

1 tablespoon oyster sauce

3 tablespoons hot water

1 cucumber, sliced
into 5cm batons

2 tablespoons caster sugar

Chinese chilli oil
(see page 18)

Don't be afraid of making these gorgeous little parcels. If you can get hold of lotus leaves, then great. If not use baking parchment paper in place of the leaves. The more you practice, the better these will taste. This is the same for any dish – it's about having confidence in the kitchen. And it's OK to mess up. When you do get it right, it's really satisfying. We spend a hell of a lot of time eating in our lives so experiment – don't just stick to dishes you know, have a go at new things and have fun with it. My dad and my whole family have taught me that.

1. Rinse the rice, then put it into a saucepan with a tight-fitting lid. Add the water and bring to the boil over a medium to high heat. Once boiling, put the lid on the pan and reduce the heat to very low. Continue to cook for 5 minutes. Remove the pan from the heat and leave it to stand for a minimum of 10 minutes. Do not remove the lid until 10 minutes is up. Put the rice to one side.

2. Drain the shiitake mushrooms, then chop them into roughly 1cm pieces. Heat the oil in a wok over a high heat. Add both types of mushrooms, garlic, ginger, spring onions and peanuts. Fry for about 1 minute, then add the dried scallops to the wok, if using.

3. Pour in the Shaoxing rice wine, soy sauce, fish sauce, oyster sauce and hot water. Lower the heat and simmer for a further 3–5 minutes, until the liquid has almost evaporated. Remove from the heat.

4. Remove the lid from the rice pot and scrape the cooked mushroom mixture on to the rice. Mix together thoroughly, taste and add a little more soy sauce if necessary.

5. Take the lotus leaves out of the water and cut each one in half with scissors, removing the woody stalk.

6. Divide the rice into six portions. Spoon a portion of the mixture on to the bottom third of a lotus leaf half. Draw in the sides, folding them over the rice, then roll the leaf over itself away from you. Your rice should now be tightly encased within the leaf. Place the package in a large steamer basket with the joins facing down. Repeat with the remaining leaves and rice mixture. Steam the parcels over a high heat for 10–20 minutes.

7. Carefully remove the parcels and peel back the sides to reveal the rice inside. Don't eat the lotus leaves! Serve with the cucumber batons dipped in a little sugar and Chinese chilli oil.

# 17. **STEAMED RICE PARCELS WITH CHINESE MUSHROOMS**

200g minced chicken

2 tablespoons leek,
very finely chopped

1 spring onion,
finely chopped

a 1–2cm piece of fresh
ginger, peeled and grated or
very finely chopped

2 teaspoons sesame oil,
or to taste

1 teaspoon Shaoxing
rice wine or dry sherry

salt and ground white pepper

1 egg, separated

cornflour, for dusting

12 round white wonton
wrappers (see page 23)

1 tablespoon groundnut oil

**For the dipping sauce**

2 tablespoons runny honey

1 tablespoon light soy sauce

1 tablespoon chopped
fresh chives

150ml water

Have you ever gone out to eat dim sum and wondered, 'How do they make these? They taste so amazing, they must be complicated' as you marvelled at the wonderful steaming baskets of joy? I know I have. Well, let me assure you, with a little practice you can become your very own dim sum chef. Like most Chinese food, it's all about the preparation. Most dim sum dumplings are wrapped in a pastry of some description and, luckily, you can buy ready-made, rolled and cut pastry in most good Chinese supermarkets or online. Once you have this vital ingredient then the rest is just down to your imagination. Chicken, pork, prawns, minced beef . . . freestyle your way around the fridge and create the fillings you want. Try this delicious and super-easy recipe, or the Pork and Prawn Potstickers on page 72 – tasty, healthy and really fun to make!

1. Put the chicken, leek, spring onion and ginger into a bowl or on to a board, and mix together well, adding the sesame oil, Shaoxing rice wine and a pinch of salt and pepper. Add a little egg white if the mixture needs binding together.

2. Dust a work surface with cornflour and lay out the wonton wrappers. Place a small spoonful of the chicken mixture in the middle of a wrapper and brush the outside rim lightly with egg yolk.

3. Fold over the wrapper to make a half-moon shape, enclosing the filling inside. Press out any air bubbles and seal the join, pinching the ends shut at the rim. Repeat with the remaining wonton wrappers and chicken mixture.

4. Heat a non-stick frying pan with deep sides, or a wok, over a medium to high heat. Add a glug of oil and place the dumplings in the pan. If using a wok, arrange them around the bottom and lower sides. Cook for 30–60 seconds over a medium heat, until crisp and dark golden on the base. Then pour in enough water to create steam around the dumplings (about 200ml) at the base of the wok or pan. Cover the pan and steam the dumplings for 5–8 minutes (topping up the water if the pan is drying out), or until the filling is cooked through.

5. To make the dipping sauce, mix together the runny honey and soy sauce in a small bowl. Sprinkle in the chives to garnish.

6. Remove the potstickers from the pan and serve coloured side up, with the dipping sauce on the side.

# 18. CHICKEN AND LEEK MAGIC POTSTICKERS

PREPARATION TIME 20 MINUTES    COOKING TIME 10 MINUTES

**MAKES 8**

80g minced pork

1 clove of garlic, peeled and finely chopped

2 spring onions, finely sliced

a 2cm piece of fresh ginger, peeled and finely chopped

1 tablespoon Shaoxing rice wine or dry sherry

1 teaspoon sesame oil

1 teaspoon fish sauce

2 tablespoons light soy sauce

salt and ground white pepper

1 egg yolk

8 medium-sized prawns, shells removed, the tails left on

8 gyoza dumpling wrappers (see page 21)

2 tablespoons groundnut oil

150ml water

These are classic old-style wok-fried and steamed dumplings, filled with love and happiness. Sticky, gooey and full of fantastic flavours, the method of making them has probably not changed for thousands of years. One of the joys of creating them is the organized chaos – all the chopping and mixing of the filling gets bound up in neat, ordered little parcels. Chaos dumplings! Make them in the afternoon, put them in the fridge, put the kids to bed, get your girlfriends round, put your wok on to cook them and then sit down for a good gossip. That's what I do (minus the kids!).

1. Mix together all of the ingredients, apart from the egg yolk, prawns, dumpling wrappers and groundnut oil, squeezing the mixture together between your fingers to attain a smooth consistency.

2. Place one of the gyoza wrappers on the palm of your hand and spoon an eighth of the mixture into the centre of the wrapper, leaving a 1½cm border.

3. Push one of the prawns into the middle of the pork mix. Most of the prawn should lie within the pastry shell, with the tail poking out of the edge.

4. Brush the edge of the pastry disc with the egg yolk and carefully bring together the two sides of the pastry to create a half-moon shape with the prawn tail poking out of one side. Place on a lightly greased board. Repeat the process with the remaining mixture, prawns and wrappers.

5. Heat the oil in a large frying pan with a lid on a medium to high heat. Once hot, add the dumplings and fry for 2 minutes until the base has turned brown and become crisp. Carefully pour in 100ml of water and quickly place the lid on the frying pan. Be careful of the mixture of water and hot oil, though, as it can cause flames.

6. Leave the dumplings to steam with the lid on for 2 minutes. Remove the lid and check how much water remains – there should only be a dribble left. Add a further 50ml and replace the lid, then steam for another 3 minutes.

7. Turn off the heat and serve the dumplings immediately.

PREPARATION TIME 20 MINUTES    COOKING TIME 15 MINUTES

# I9. **PORK AND PRAWN POTSTICKERS**

**SERVES 4**

12 raw king prawns, peeled,
de-veined and finely chopped
to the texture of mince

8 water chestnuts, chopped
into 0.5cm pieces

2 teaspoons toasted sesame oil

salt and ground white pepper

4 tablespoons sesame seeds

6 tablespoons groundnut oil

a 2cm piece of fresh ginger,
peeled and finely chopped

1 clove of garlic, peeled and
very finely sliced

3 spring onions, very finely
sliced into rounds

2 cucumbers, roughly peeled,
deseeded and chopped into
2cm chunks

1 tablespoon fish sauce

2 teaspoons rice vinegar

1 tablespoon light soy sauce

**To serve**

Chinese chilli oil
(see page 18)

Forget the stodgy deep-fried bread of traditional sesame prawn toast, try this simple but delicious method of cooking prawns instead. The water chestnuts provide a crunchy texture and the vinegar-enhanced fried cucumber turns this simple dish into a knock out treat.

1. Put the prawns, water chestnuts and sesame oil into a bowl and mix together. Season with a pinch of salt and white pepper.

2. Spoon the sesame seeds on to a flat tray or plate. Take an eighth of the mixture and lightly shape it into a small ball. Roll the mixture in the sesame seeds so that all sides are coated. Flatten out the ball to form a small patty shape, then place on a lightly oiled plate. Repeat the process with the remaining mixture.

3. Heat 4 tablespoons of the groundnut oil in a large frying pan over a medium to high heat. When hot, add the patties and cook for about 2 minutes on each side. The seeds will turn a lovely golden brown but be careful that they don't overcook as they will taste bitter if they do. When cooked, remove the patties and place on kitchen paper to soak up any excess oil. Leave in a warm place while you prepare the stir-fry.

4. Heat the remaining 2 tablespoons of oil in a wok over a high heat. When hot, add the ginger, garlic and spring onions. Stir-fry for 2 minutes before adding in the diced cucumber pieces. Continue to stir-fry for a further minute, then pour in the fish sauce, rice vinegar and soy sauce, and stir to incorporate.

5. Spoon the cucumber mixture on to a plate, top with the prawn balls and serve with chilli oil.

PREPARATION TIME 15 MINUTES    COOKING TIME 10 MINUTES

# 20. SESAME PRAWN BALLS WITH STIR-FRIED CUCUMBERS

500g minced beef

a 3cm piece of fresh ginger, peeled and finely chopped

2 cloves of garlic, peeled and finely chopped

a small bunch of fresh coriander, leaves and stalks finely chopped

a pinch of Chinese five-spice powder

1½ tablespoons light soy sauce

1½ tablespoons Shaoxing rice wine or dry sherry

salt and ground white pepper

1 carrot, peeled and chopped into roughly 1cm-thick rounds

To serve

Chinese chilli oil (see page 18)

light soy sauce

The beauty of dim sum is that you get the opportunity to travel thousands of miles across Asia in one mealtime, just order as much as you like and revel in a journey of the tastebuds. These beef balls can be made in advance and steamed to order when you are ready to eat. Simply store them, covered in cling film, in a single layer on a tray or plate in the fridge for up to two days. Serve with two or three other dim sum dishes from this chapter, or simply on their own as a super-healthy and tasty snack. A classic dim sum treat.

1. Put the minced beef, ginger, garlic, coriander, five-spice powder, soy sauce and Shaoxing rice wine into a bowl and mix together, using your hands. Squeeze the mixture together to break down the minced beef. Mix well and season generously with salt and pepper.

2. Form the mixture into walnut-sized balls, using your hands. (You can oil your hands with groundnut oil first, if you like.) Place the balls onto a slice of carrot, then put on a plate and chill in the fridge for 30 minutes to firm up, if you have the time.

3. Place the carrot slices and beef balls directly into a bamboo steamer basket. Place the steamer over a wok of boiling water, ensuring that the base of the steamer does not touch the water. Steam for 10 minutes, or until the beef balls are cooked through and firm (steam them in batches if necessary).

4. Remove the steamer from the wok, being careful to keep any cooking juices on the plates. Serve immediately, while still steaming hot, with Chinese chilli oil and soy sauce for dipping.

PREPARATION TIME 15 MINUTES    COOKING TIME 10–15 MINUTES

# 21. **STEAMED BEEF AND CORIANDER BALLS**

**SERVES 4**

250g rice (a short-grain
Asian style rice works best)

2.5 litres water

Show me a Chinese person who doesn't love congee and I will demand a blood test, because this dish is the Chinese food rite of passage. Traditionally a way of using up leftover rice, it has developed into a dish of its own. Comparable to rice pudding or tapioca, congee is often eaten for breakfast, either in its purest form with just a dash of soy sauce, or jazzed up with dried scallops, fried onions and ginger. However you decide to eat congee, once you try it you'll fall in love. Momma Wan's congee is absolutely the best in the world and you can be assured that any time I go home for the weekend I put in my order at the Family Wan Chinese Takeaway!

1. Wash the rice in a sieve until the water runs clear (this is not completely necessary, but if you have time it is recommended).

2. Put the washed rice in a large saucepan. Cover with the water and bring to the boil. Reduce the heat to a simmer and cook for at least 40 minutes, stirring occasionally to ensure none of the rice sticks to the bottom and subsequently burns.

3. The amount of water can vary depending on cooking times and the interpretation of simmering, so if you feel that the dish needs more water then add it. This is a very forgiving dish, which is almost impossible to overcook – it is not uncommon to see a pot of congee simmering away for several hours in a Chinese house; the only care needed is an occasional stir and the addition of water.

## BASIC ACCOMPANIMENTS

| | |
|---|---|
| Chinese pickled vegetables | red chilli |
| fermented tofu | Chinese sausage |
| light soy sauce | boiled egg |
| peanuts | smoked mackerel |
| dried scallops | salted fish |
| dried prawns | steamed fish |
| spring onions | poached chicken |

PREPARATION TIME 2 MINUTES    COOKING TIME 40 MINUTES MINIMUM

**SERVES 4**

100g minced pork

a 1cm piece of fresh ginger,
peeled and finely diced

2 spring onions, one finely
sliced, the other shredded
into 4cm lengths

2 tablespoons light soy sauce

1 teaspoon fish sauce

2 teaspoons sesame oil

6 eggs

salt and ground white pepper

1 fresh red chilli, deseeded
and finely sliced

**To serve**

toast

chilli sauce

This is a bit like a Chinese version of sausages and eggs. The pork balls are packed with flavours that mark them out from your average banger, and the steaming process ensures that this dish is reasonably guilt-free eating.

1. Place the minced pork, ginger, sliced spring onion, 1 tablespoon of soy sauce, the fish sauce and sesame oil in a bowl and mix together thoroughly.

2. Divide the mixture into 8 and roll into small balls.

3. Crack the eggs into a shallow bowl that will fit inside a large steamer basket, being careful not to break the yolks. The eggs should overlap a little, but should form a single layer. Drizzle the eggs with the remaining tablespoon of soy sauce and season to taste.

4. Carefully place the pork balls on top of the eggs, dotting them around randomly, but being careful not to break the yolks.

5. Place the bowl in your steamer basket and steam over hot water for 20–25 minutes. The pork balls should be cooked through and the egg whites set, whilst the egg yolks should still be slightly runny.

6. Carefully remove the bowl from the steamer. Sprinkle with the shredded spring onion and sliced chilli and serve with toast and your favourite chilli sauce.

PREPARATION TIME 15 MINUTES     COOKING TIME 20–25 MINUTES

# 23. STEAMED EGG WITH PORK BALLS

6 eggs

2 tablespoons light soy sauce

2 teaspoons toasted sesame oil

2 spring onions, finely sliced
into rounds

salt and ground white pepper

12 ready-cooked tiger prawns,
peeled and de-veined

Sesame oil, soy sauce and eggs are a wonderful combination. Balanced by the natural sweetness of fresh prawns, this is a delicious variation on the Western omelette.

1. Boil the kettle to prepare the water for the steamer.

2. Crack the eggs into a bowl and roughly whisk. Add the soy sauce, sesame oil, spring onions and seasoning. Whisk again so that all the ingredients are thoroughly combined.

3. Place the prawns in the bottom of a large shallow bowl, or into individual ramekins, then pour over the beaten egg mixture and place the dishes in a large steamer basket. Steam the eggs over boiling water for 12–15 minutes until just set.

4. Remove from the steamer, mop up any condensation and serve as part of a larger meal.

PREPARATION TIME 5 MINUTES    COOKING TIME 12–15 MINUTES

# 24. STEAMED EGG WITH PRAWNS

**For the char siu filling**

2 tablespoons groundnut oil

200g pork tenderloin,
roughly diced into 1cm pieces

2 tablespoons Shaoxing
rice wine or dry sherry

1 tablespoon yellow bean paste

1 tablespoon hoisin sauce

1 tablespoon light soy sauce

**For the buns**

500g plain flour, plus
a little extra for dusting

1 sachet (7g) of
fast-action yeast

2 tablespoons groundnut oil

2 tablespoons caster sugar

300ml warm water

1 tablespoon sesame oil

**To garnish**

16 goji berries (optional)

In Chinese cuisine there are so many different types of dumpling, with so many different fillings and flavours inside them; whether steamed, fried or boiled, the Chinese have eaten them for thousands of years. These buns filled with barbecued pork are a classic dim sum dumpling. You can make a vegetarian version by using the mushroom filling on page 88.

1. Heat the oil in a wok over a high heat. Once hot, add the diced pork and stir-fry until it turns golden. Pour in the Shaoxing rice wine and let it reduce for 30 seconds. Spoon in the yellow bean paste and the hoisin sauce, and stir to incorporate. Add the soy sauce and turn off the heat. Let the mixture sit and cool while you make the buns.

2. Put all the ingredients apart from the water and sesame oil into a bowl and roughly combine. Pour half the warm water into the dry ingredients and stir. Pour in the remaining water and mix well. Dust a clean surface with a little of the extra flour, and tip the dough on to it. Knead with your hands for 5 minutes. Once kneaded, if possible try to shape your dough into a rough 'bun'.

3. Rub the inside of a large bowl with the sesame oil. Put in your dough, cover with clingfilm or a clean teatowel, place in a warm place and leave to prove until the dough has at least doubled in size. This normally takes a minimum of 90 minutes.

4. Tip the dough on to a floured surface and knead it again, to knock out the air. Take a golfball-sized piece of dough and flatten it with the palm of your hand. Spoon a heaped tablespoon of the cooled pork mixture into the middle of the flattened pastry. Carefully pull up the edges of the dough to encase the filling in a ball shape, then smooth the edges and place on a floured tray.

5. Repeat the process with the remaining dough and filling, then cover the buns with a damp tea towel and leave to rise for another 15 minutes. Once risen, place each one on a small disc of baking parchment with the join underneath. Top each bun with 2 goji berries, if using. Place in a steamer and cook for 12–15 minutes.

6. Take the steamer baskets to the table and serve immediately, as part of a dim sum feast.

PREPARATION TIME 2 HOURS    COOKING TIME 20 MINUTES

**SERVES 4**

40g dried shiitake
mushrooms, soaked in warm
water for 10 minutes

2 tablespoons groundnut oil

2 cloves of garlic,
peeled and finely sliced

2 spring onions,
finely sliced into rounds

1 fresh red chilli, deseeded
and finely diced

20g chestnut mushrooms,
finely chopped

30g oyster mushrooms,
finely chopped

2 tablespoons Shaoxing
rice wine or dry sherry

1 tablespoon light soy sauce

1 tablespoon oyster sauce

cornflour, for dusting

8–12 wonton wrappers
(see page 23)

a little water

1 tablespoon sesame oil

Experienced dim sum chefs in restaurants will spend a long time making fanciful shapes with their dumplings, but there is no need to do that at home. Try making these vegetarian steamed dumplings at the same time as the buns filled with char siu pork on page 86 and serve up a whole tableful of different tastes.

1. Drain the shiitake mushrooms through a sieve, being careful to retain the liquid. Roughly chop the mushooms into very small pieces.

2. Heat the groundnut oil over a high heat in a wok. Once hot, add the garlic, spring onions and red chilli. Stir-fry for 1 minute before adding the chopped mushrooms, then continue to stir-fry for 2–3 minutes.

3. Reduce the heat to medium and stir in the Shaoxing rice wine, soy sauce, oyster sauce and 100ml of the reserved shiitake liquid. Continue cooking for 2–3 minutes until the liquid has reduced to almost nothing and the mushrooms have become tender. Turn the heat off under the wok and leave the mixture to cool to room temperature. This can be made the day before and left in the fridge overnight.

4. Dust a clean surface with cornflour and lay your wrappers on top. Carefully place 1–2 teaspoons of the mixture into the middle of one of the wrappers. Dip your finger in some water and wet the rim of the wrapper all the way around. Gather up all sides of the wrapper and scrunch them together so the parcel looks like a small 'money bag'.

5. Smear the sesame oil on to a plate that will fit in your steamer and place your finished dumpling on the plate.

6. Repeat the process with the remaining mixture and dumpling wrappers, then place the plate inside your steamer and steam over boiling water for 5–8 minutes until the dumpling has cooked through.

7. Serve as part of a larger dim sum meal.

PREPARATION TIME 30 MINUTES    COOKING TIME 15 MINUTES

# 26. STEAMED MUSHROOM DUMPLINGS

'COOK WITH ALL YOUR HEART SO FAMILY
AND FRIENDS WILL NEVER BE FAR AWAY'

# 3

# FAVOURITE
# FAMILY WAN
# DISHES

The Family Wan dishes are so close to my heart
– I grew up learning them from Dad and am so
proud to have them here in this book. You will
find other recipes of Dad's throughout the book,
but this chapter includes those, like the Simple
Soy-glazed Chicken and the Spicy Cucumber and
Spring Onion Salad, that remind me of home.

6 cleaned scallops with roes attached, shells washed

a 3cm piece of fresh ginger, peeled and cut into matchsticks

2 spring onions, trimmed and cut into matchsticks

salt and ground white pepper

1 teaspoon sesame oil

**For the burning oil sauce (see pictures on pages 108–9)**

1 fresh red chilli, finely sliced

½ a spring onion, finely sliced

1–2 cloves of garlic, peeled and finely chopped

1 tablespoon light soy sauce

½–1 tablespoon fish sauce

½ teaspoon sesame oil

75ml groundnut oil

Chopsticks were invented before forks, and hands were around before chopsticks – and never will eating with your fingers feel so satisfying as tucking into this dish. It conjures up memories for me of total food euphoria, as Dad would usually cook this for us as a tastebud teaser, flirting with our hunger before we eventually devoured a 25-million-course family meal! Dad's inner showman would take centre stage as he dramatically ladled the chilli oil into the soy sauce, creating an explosion of spitting oil accompanied by a firecracker soundtrack. The smell of frying chillies would engulf the room as we drenched our seafood in sauce which danced around our senses. Result: simplistic food harmony.

1. Place each scallop along with its roe into the deeper half of its shell. Divide and sprinkle over the ginger and spring onion (making sure there is an equal mix of green and white parts in each shell), and season with a little pepper and a pinch of salt.

2. Place the scallops in their half shells into a large bamboo steamer and spoon just a few drops of water over each scallop if they are very small. Cover with a lid and steam over a wok of boiling water for 6–7 minutes (depending on size) or until just cooked through.

3. Meanwhile, make the burning oil sauce. Mix together the chilli, spring onion, garlic, soy sauce, fish sauce and sesame oil in a heatproof serving bowl. Pour the groundnut oil into a pan and heat until smoking, then very carefully pour over the chilli mix, watching out for hot oil splashes. Once the oil has calmed down, mix everything together.

4. Serve the cooked scallops in their shells, being careful to retain all the liquid. Serve with the burning oil sauce on the side to spoon over, and eat immediately.

PREPARATION TIME 10 MINUTES    COOKING TIME 8–10 MINUTES

# 27. DRAGON SCALLOPS WITH BURNING OIL SAUCE

2 eggs

salt and ground white pepper

2 spring onions,
trimmed and finely chopped

2 tablespoons groundnut oil

a 1cm piece of fresh ginger,
peeled and chopped

1 or 2 cloves of garlic, peeled
and finely chopped

½–1 tablespoon chilli bean
paste (see page 18), to taste

2 teaspoons fish sauce

½ teaspoon rice vinegar
or cider vinegar

1 teaspoon oyster sauce

a pinch of caster sugar

500g firm tofu, drained
and cut into 2cm cubes

½–1 fresh red chilli,
deseeded and finely chopped

'Food dreaming' is one of my favourite pastimes. Whether I'm on set filming a show, sitting by the river or even in a meeting, you can guarantee it won't be long before my mind drifts off to my virtual dinner table. I can spend hours remembering food I ate as a child, food I've eaten whilst travelling around Asia and, of course, the amazing food that Dad cooked me. For me, food dreaming is a wonderful way to remember happy times and the people in my life I love and miss. Eating Nan's roast potatoes on a rare Sunday visit or sharing a plate of *popiah* – delicious Malaysian stuffed pancakes – with my best friend in a hawker's market in Singapore are treasured memories. The beauty of food dreaming is you can eat as much as you like and you never get full!

1. Beat the eggs in a bowl and season with a little salt and pepper. Add 1 teaspoon of the chopped spring onion and set aside.

2. Heat a wok over a medium heat and add a dash of oil. Add the ginger and garlic and cook for 10 seconds. Add the chilli bean paste and cook over the heat until aromatic. Add 4–5 tablespoons of hot water and stir to mix well into the chilli bean paste. Flavour with the fish sauce, vinegar, oyster sauce and the pinch of sugar. Bring to a simmer, then taste and adjust the flavouring as necessary. Add the tofu pieces and stir gently to coat them in the sauce. Cover with a lid and leave to steam braise for 5 minutes.

3. Meanwhile heat a medium non-stick frying pan over a high heat. Add a dash of oil and swirl it around to coat the pan. Once the oil is hot, add half of the beaten egg and spread it out to the edges of the pan. Leave on the heat until almost cooked through and golden underneath, with crisp edges. Turn over and cook on the other side, until golden and a little crisp. Remove from the pan and drain on kitchen paper. Repeat this stage for the second omelette.

4. To serve, spoon the tofu over each omelette. Garnish with the rest of the spring onion and the chilli. To eat, roll up the omelettes around the tofu and slice into pieces, or eat as it is.

PREPARATION TIME 10 MINUTES    COOKING TIME 15 MINUTES

# 28. **MY MA-PO TOFU WITH CHINESE OMELETTE**

3 tablespoons groundnut oil

6 chicken thighs, on the bone, skin removed

2 cloves of garlic, peeled and finely sliced

a 2cm piece of fresh ginger, peeled and finely sliced

3 spring onions: 2 finely sliced into rounds, 1 sliced into long diagonal pieces

6 tablespoons water

1 tablespoon honey

5 tablespoons light soy sauce

½ a fresh red chilli, finely sliced

Food has always been at the heart of my family, whether we were cooking it and eating it ourselves, or whether we were dishing-up for our customers in the restaurant. I have to say that my dad is the best Chinese chef in the entire world and this soy chicken recipe of his is based on a traditional old-school, Hong Kong–Chinese dish. His version is much quicker to make; it's a little more Westernized and easy to knock up in a domestic kitchen. It goes amazingly with the Spicy Cucumber and Spring Onion Salad on page 98.

1. Heat 2 tablespoons of oil in a large wok over a high heat. When hot, add the chicken thighs and brown them all over. This will take approximately 4–5 minutes. Once browned, remove and set aside.

2. Reduce the heat to medium and add the remaining oil. Once warmed through, add the garlic, ginger and the 2 finely sliced spring onions. Fry for 2–3 minutes, until just softening. Put the chicken back into the wok and toss to incorporate with the rest of the ingredients.

3. Pour in the water, honey and soy sauce. Increase the heat and bring to the boil. Once boiling, put a lid on the wok (if you don't have a lid big enough, cover it with foil) and cook for 5 minutes.

4. Remove the lid and turn the chicken thighs. They should be nicely caramelized in the reduced liquid by now. Continue to cook for another 3 minutes, until the liquid has reduced to a sticky glaze and the chicken thighs have become gloriously dark and glossy. Remove the chicken from the pan and allow to rest for 3 minutes.

5. Place the chicken thighs on a serving plate and garnish with the remaining spring onion and the red chilli.

PREPARATION TIME 5 MINUTES    COOKING TIME 15–20 MINUTES

## 30. SPICY CUCUMBER AND SPRING ONION SALAD

**SERVES 4**

1 cucumber, roughly peeled

1 clove of garlic, peeled and finely chopped

½ a fresh red chilli, finely sliced

2 spring onions, finely sliced

3 tablespoons rice vinegar

1 teaspoon sesame oil

1 teaspoon fish sauce

1 teaspoon light soy sauce

1 teaspoon caster sugar

a pinch of salt

Love, love, love this little salad! It may not look much but it packs a zingy punch in each mouthful. It is the perfect accessory to any dinner outfit that you're putting together on the table. Particularly good when sashaying down a catwalk next to the Simple Soy-glazed Chicken (see page 96).

1. Slice the tip off each end of the cucumber. Cut the cucumber in half. Slice each half lengthways down the middle, then using a teaspoon scoop out the seeds and discard.

2. Slice the cucumber into long, angled strips about 0.5cm thick. Put them into a bowl with the garlic, chilli and spring onions.

3. In a separate bowl mix together the remaining ingredients to form a dressing. Pour the dressing over the cucumber mixture and leave to sit for 2 minutes before serving.

PREPARATION TIME 5 MINUTES

# 31. CARROT SALAD WITH SESAME SEEDS

**SERVES 4**

3–4 medium carrots,
washed and peeled

2 teaspoons sesame seeds

2 tablespoons soy sauce

2 tablespoons rice vinegar

2 tablespoons sesame oil

1 teaspoon caster sugar

There is no mistaking that at a Chinese dinner table balance, or yin and yang, is uber-important. A quick way to achieve balance with a meal is to add an effortless surprise, and salads can do just that, subtly and with total confidence. Chinese salads and garnishes tend to be sharp and simple, more often than not quite sour. They are a brilliant way to add texture to both heavy meat dishes or very light fish dishes. Serve this salad on the side and add just a little to every other mouthful; you'll be transported into a whole new mealtime experience.

1. Coarsely grate the carrots and put them in a serving bowl.

2. Put your wok on a medium heat. When hot, add the sesame seeds and toast until golden. This will only take a couple of minutes – keep them moving in the wok so they don't burn.

3. To make the dressing, mix together the soy sauce, vinegar, oil, sugar and toasted sesame seeds, then pour the dressing over the carrot. Toss the salad with your hands so that each piece of carrot is coated in dressing.

4. The salad can be refrigerated for up to 2 days before serving.

PREPARATION TIME 10 MINUTES

**SERVES 1–2**

750ml chicken stock

2 tablespoons oyster sauce

2 spring onions, whites bruised, greens chopped

a 4cm piece of fresh ginger, one half peeled and cut into matchsticks, the other half unpeeled and bruised

1 clove of garlic, peeled and bruised

salt and ground white pepper

1 tablespoon groundnut oil

100g pork loin/tenderloin, very thinly sliced

1 teaspoon light soy sauce

1–2 bunches of mature spinach, stalks removed, or 100g baby spinach, washed, a quarter of the leaves shredded

In the kitchen of every Chinese restaurant, woks will be lined up on the range, each one cooking away madly to get the food ready for all the customers who are waiting. Usually there will be a large pot right in the middle of all the woks: the Emperor. This is the main stockpot, and bubbling away in it will be bits of prawns, or meat, or vegetables. Using up the bits of food you don't need in a dish to prepare a stock allows you to fully appreciate and respect the food that you're making. Stocks can be frozen and used as a base to make so many other things, such as this delicious pork and ginger soup. Amazing!

1. Put the stock into a pan and add the oyster sauce, the bruised whites of the spring onions, the bashed ginger and the bruised garlic. Season with salt and pepper and bring to a gentle simmer.

2. Meanwhile heat a wok over a high heat and add a dash of oil. Add the pork and soy sauce and stir-fry, cooking very quickly until sealed on both sides.

3. Place the whole spinach leaves in serving bowls. Top with the pork. Pour over the stock (removing the bruised pieces if you like) and garnish with the shredded spinach, matchsticked ginger and spring onion greens.

PREPARATION TIME 5 MINUTES    COOKING TIME 10 MINUTES

# 32. **HEALTH, WEALTH AND HAPPINESS PORK AND GINGER SOUP**

6 dried shiitake mushrooms, soaked in warm water for a minimum of 10 minutes

2 tablespoons black beans, soaked in warm water for 5 minutes

2 tablespoons groundnut oil

3 cloves of garlic, peeled and finely sliced

1 fresh red chilli, finely diced (if you don't like it hot then remove the seeds from the chilli)

a 3cm piece of fresh ginger, peeled and finely diced

4 spring onions, sliced into 2cm rounds

3 tablespoons Shaoxing rice wine or dry sherry

3 tablespoons light soy sauce

2 tablespoons dark soy sauce

400g tofu, drained and cut into 2cm cubes

2 tablespoons chopped fresh coriander

I *love* tofu and would stand up in a culinary court and argue its case as one of the most diverse but under-used ingredients. When cooking tofu you need to respect the shyness of its flavour. It never wants to stand out from the crowd but will always surprise you when you least expect it! Black beans are wonderful with tofu as they are strong and salty in taste, adding layers of flavour. Don't overdo the salt – allow the bitterness of the beans to embrace and uplift the placid nature of the tofu in this dish.

1. Drain the shiitake mushrooms through a sieve placed over a clean bowl. Reserve 150ml of the soaking liquor. Chop the mushrooms roughly into small dice.

2. Drain the black beans and put to one side.

3. Heat the oil in a wok over a medium to high heat. Add the garlic, chilli, ginger and spring onions. Stir-fry the vegetables for 2 minutes. Add the drained and chopped mushrooms, and continue to stir-fry for a further 2 minutes before adding the drained black beans, reserved mushroom liquor, Shaoxing rice wine and both soy sauces. Bring the mixture to the boil and simmer for 2–3 minutes.

4. Add the tofu to the mixture and gently incorporate. Cook the tofu through in the sauce for 3–4 minutes until very tender. Sprinkle with the chopped coriander

5. Serve as part of a larger meal or simply with plain rice for a healthy vegetarian option.

PREPARATION TIME 20 MINUTES    COOKING TIME 10 MINUTES

# 33. BLACK BEANS AND TOFU

**SERVES 4**

4 tablespoons groundnut oil

4 x 175g pollock fillets,
skin on but scaled

2 green peppers, deseeded
and cut into 2cm chunks

1 small pineapple, peeled and
cut into 2cm chunks

100g sugar

5 tablespoons white
wine vinegar

3 tablespoons tomato ketchup

2 tablespoons light soy sauce

I like the idea that my Chinese ancestors came up with the whole idea of sweet and sour flavours working together. It's an amazing combination. Served with some plain rice and boiled greens, this dish is just amazing. These flavours match perfectly with fish and this recipe is a super-healthy version of the 'gloopy' sweet and sour sauce that you are probably used to having from your local takeaway. Make this once and you won't want to go back . . .

1. Heat half the oil in a frying pan over a medium to high heat. When it's hot, add the fish, skin-side down, and fry for 4–5 minutes. The skin should be crisp, but not burnt.

2. Flip the fish over and fry for a further 4–5 minutes. The fish should now be cooked through, but if needed you can put the pan into a 200°C oven to finish off. When cooked, remove it from the frying pan and set aside.

3. Wipe the frying pan clean and put it back on a medium heat. Add the remaining oil. Once hot, add the green pepper and fry for 2–3 minutes, until the pepper just begins to soften. Add the pineapple and toss together.

4. Quickly add the sugar and spread it evenly over the base of the pan. Leave it to caramelize for 2–3 minutes, without stirring. Don't let the sugar burn.

5. When you have a thick caramel, carefully pour in the vinegar – it will bubble and may well spit a little. Stir everything well, then remove the sauce from the heat and add the tomato ketchup and soy sauce. Stir again. You may need to add a little water at this point if the sauce is too thick.

6. Add the fish to the sweet and sour sauce and stir gently to coat, or serve as a dipping sauce alongside the fish.

PREPARATION TIME 10 MINUTES    COOKING TIME 25–30 MINUTES

**SERVES 2**

2 tablespoons groundnut oil

250g ho fun noodles
(see page 21), soaked and
drained according to
packet instructions

salt and ground white pepper

6 raw king prawns,
peeled and de-veined

1 medium (200g) squid,
cleaned and cut into strips

4 medium scallops out
of their shells, cleaned
and roes removed

4 Chinese fried fish balls
(see page 18, optional)

1–1½ tablespoons oyster sauce

½–1 tablespoon light
soy sauce

200ml prawn-shell or
fish stock (see page 124)

2 tablespoons sliced bamboo
shoots, drained

3 water chestnuts,
roughly chopped

1 teaspoon sesame oil

**To serve**

Chinese chilli oil
(see page 18)

I never learned how to speak Chinese as a child. Dad was always very busy with the restaurant so he didn't really have time to teach me his native tongue. On occasion, my sister, brother and I were sent to Chinese school but that didn't last long as I was far too naughty and spent most of my time sitting under the table looking up the girls' skirts! As a result, the only Chinese phrases I knew, used or recognized were associated with eating. *Sit Fan* (rice dinner), *Sit Mein* (noodle dinner), *Sit Mem Bo* (bread dinner), *Sit Bao* (full up). The last phrase wasn't used very often! This meant that as I got older, food became the way that Dad and I communicated about his culture. Being able to ask for food in Chinese was so important to me, not just because I was hungry but because it gave me precious moments with Dad when he was able to teach me about himself, his life before England and his life before me. Enjoy this recipe – ho fun to your heart's content!

1. Heat a wok over a high heat. Add a dash of oil and heat, then add the ho fun noodles and stir-fry for a minute to cook them through, seasoning them with a little salt and pepper. Remove from the wok and leave to one side.

2. Heat the wok again, adding another dash of oil. Stir-fry the prawns, squid and scallops for 30 seconds. Add the fish balls, if using, along with the oyster sauce, soy sauce and stock, and cover, leaving everything to cook over a medium heat for 2–3 minutes, stirring occasionally. Once the squid, prawns and scallops are just cooked through, remove the lid and taste, adjusting the seasoning as necessary.

3. Stir in the bamboo shoots and water chestnuts and let them warm through for 1–2 minutes. Add the ho fun noodles and mix together gently, allowing the noodles to absorb the liquid but being careful not to overcook them.

4. Finish with a dash of sesame oil sprinkled over to taste. Divide the seafood equally between the plates and serve with a little Chinese chilli oil on the side.

PREPARATION TIME 15 MINUTES     COOKING TIME 10 MINUTES

## 35. DAD'S FRIED HO FUN NOODLES WITH MIXED SEAFOOD

1–2 bunches Chinese lettuce
(see page 18), leaves separated
and washed really well to
remove grit

2 tablespoons groundnut oil

1 clove of garlic,
peeled and chopped

1 heaped tablespoon dried
shrimp (see page 20), soaked
for 15 minutes in hot water,
then roughly chopped

1 tablespoon light soy sauce

salt and ground white pepper

1 heaped tablespoon fresh,
shelled peanuts, papery inner
skin removed, chopped

There's a simple beauty about lettuce that often gets overlooked when it's banished to a lifetime of buffet side salads and BLTs. The Chinese have used lettuce in hot meals for hundreds of years; they've even cultivated their own – namely 'Chinese leaf'. Stir-frying with garlic and dried shrimps is a really easy way of introducing this elegantly versatile vegetable into your wok and on to your dinner table. Best served as an accompaniment to a dark meat or spicy dry dish, the lettuce will soak up its peppery sauce and add a touch of class and sophistication to your meal.

1. Roughly tear the larger lettuce leaves to match the size of the smaller ones.

2. Heat a wok over a medium-high heat and add a dash of oil. Once hot, stir-fry the garlic, moving it around in the pan for 30 seconds until aromatic. Add the dried shrimp and stir with the garlic for a couple of seconds, then add all the lettuce and stir over the heat until it has wilted.

3. Season with soy sauce and a pinch of pepper. Taste and adjust the seasoning if necessary. Scatter in the peanuts, mix and serve immediately.

PREPARATION TIME 20 MINUTES    COOKING TIME 5 MINUTES

# 36. **STIR-FRIED CHINESE LETTUCE WITH DRIED SHRIMP AND PEANUTS**

# 37. QUICK COOK BEANSPROUTS WITH DRIED SHRIMP AND WHITE PEPPER

**SERVES 2**

300g beansprouts, rinsed

2 tablespoons dried shrimp (see page 20)

pinch of salt

¼ teaspoon ground white pepper

½ tablespoon light soy sauce

½ tablespoon sesame oil

Sometimes the simplest of Chinese dishes are the heroes on the dinner table. Beansprouts are beautifully delicate and will complement all meat and fish dishes. On the occasions I want a fuss-free and tasty, healthy dinner I simply serve this on top of a bowl of fluffy white rice and settle down on the sofa to channel-surf to my heart's content – pyjamas optional!

1. Soak the dried shrimp in hot water for 15 minutes, or until softened. Drain and roughly chop, then put into a bowl.

2. Bring a pan of salted water to the boil and blanch the beansprouts for 30 seconds to warm them through. Make sure you don't overcook them, as you want them to retain some bite. Drain them immediately and mix with the dried shrimp. Season with a pinch of salt and the ground white pepper, soy sauce and sesame oil.

3. Mix really well to distribute the seasoning and serve warm or cold.

PREPARATION TIME 20 MINUTES    COOKING TIME 1–2 MINUTES

1 litre fresh chicken stock

a 5cm piece of fresh ginger,
peeled and bruised

100g dried rice stick noodles
(see page 22)

2 teaspoons sesame oil

3 tablespoons oyster sauce

2 tablespoons light soy sauce

2 teaspoons fish sauce

ground white pepper

250g cooked seafood: prawns,
squid, mussels

3 spring onions, finely sliced
into rounds

To me, this dish feels like clean living in a bowl. Feel free to experiment with different combinations of seafood, and add baby spinach or broccoli to transform this simple soup into a restorative elixir.

1. Bring the chicken stock to the boil, add the ginger and leave to simmer gently while you prepare the rest of the dish.

2. Cook the noodles according to the packet instructions. (Generally, you soak them in hot water for a few minutes before draining and running cold water over them until they are cool.) Once cooked and cooled, pour over the sesame oil, mix and divide equally between two bowls.

3. Add the oyster, soy and fish sauces to the simmering stock, then season with white pepper to taste.

4. Divide the seafood between the two bowls on top of the noodles and scatter the spring onions over the seafood.

5. When ready to eat, pour the boiling stock into the bowls and leave to sit for 2 minutes before serving, to ensure the seafood is warm, and you'll then have a hearty, healthy lunch for two or a snack for four.

PREPARATION TIME 5 MINUTES    COOKING TIME 15 MINUTES

# 38. RICE STICK NOODLES AND SEAFOOD

4 tablespoons groundnut oil

400g sirloin steak,
sliced into thin strips

1 onion, peeled and diced
into medium chunks

4 cloves of garlic, peeled
and finely sliced

a 4cm piece of fresh ginger,
peeled and finely sliced

3 tomatoes, roughly chopped

200ml chicken or beef stock
(fresh or from a cube)

2 tablespoons oyster sauce

2 tablespoons soy sauce

6 tablespoons tomato ketchup

1 tablespoon sugar

salt and ground white
pepper, to season

1 tablespoon sesame oil

1 spring onion, finely shredded

Poppa Wan would cook this dish for us at the end of a night's work in the family restaurant. Full of flavour and just what you want when you're hungry and tired. The beauty of this dish is that it really is an East-meets-West kind of guy. The tomato sauce is 'China-fied' with the addition of oyster sauce and sesame oil. Fusion food at its best and most honest. Think of it as ragu with a karate kick!

1. Heat 2 tablespoons of the oil in a wok over a high heat. Once hot, add the strips of beef and stir-fry for 2–3 minutes until well browned. Remove the beef to a plate and put to one side for later.

2. Reduce the heat to medium and pour in the remaining oil. Add the onions and stir-fry for 3 minutes before adding the garlic and ginger. Continue to stir-fry for a further 2 minutes until the onion becomes tender.

3. Add the tomatoes and continue cooking for 2–3 minutes until the tomato flesh starts to collapse. Add the stock and stir whilst bringing to the boil. Once boiling, simmer for 2–3 minutes before adding the oyster sauce, soy sauce, tomato ketchup and sugar. Let the sauce simmer for 2–3 minutes.

4. Put the beef back in the wok, along with any juices that may have gathered on the plate, and simmer until the meat is warmed through.

5. Season before adding the sesame oil and garnish with the spring onions. Serve alongside a vegetable dish and rice.

PREPARATION TIME 10 MINUTES    COOKING TIME 20 MINUTES

# 39. **BEEF IN EASY TOMATO SAUCE**

600g thick belly pork,
bones removed

4–6 small yams, peeled
and cut into 1.5cm thick slices

**For the marinade**

1 tablespoon groundnut oil

3 tablespoons dark soy sauce

3–4 tablespoons brown sugar

2 pieces of red beancurd
(tinned or jarred, see
page 22), drained

3 tablespoons hoisin sauce

1 tablespoon yellow bean sauce

3–4 cloves of garlic,
peeled and finely chopped

a 3cm piece of fresh ginger,
finely chopped

2 tablespoons Shaoxing rice
wine or dry sherry

This dish would not look out of place on any Western table. Arranged neatly into an earthenware dish and roasted in the oven, it shrieks European, but the taste could not be more Asian. Pork belly dressed in an overcoat of hoisin and coupled with yam is a real taste of the Orient. If you can't get hold of yams, then try either sweet potato or butternut squash instead.

1. In a bowl large enough to hold the pork, mix the marinade ingredients together, mashing in the red bean curd with a fork, and put to one side.

2. Bring a large pan of water to the boil. Add the pork, bring back to the boil, then reduce the heat and simmer for 20 minutes. Take the pork out of the pan, drain and set aside to cool. When cool, remove the skin.

3. Cut the pork into strips, 4cm long, 1cm thick. Place them in the marinade and leave for 1–1½ hours.

4. When you are ready to cook, preheat the oven to 180°C/350°F/ gas 4. Take the pork out of the marinade. Arrange the pork and yam slices in alternate layers in a heatproof dish, spooning some marinade in between each layer, then pouring any remaining marinade over the top. Cover the dish with tinfoil, put into the oven and roast for 40 minutes, removing the cover for the final 15 minutes.

5. Serve the yams and pork spooned over rice.

PREPARATION TIME 1½–2 HOURS    COOKING TIME 40 MINUTES

# 40. PORK AND YAMS

SAU TAO SHRIMP NOODLES(563)　　　SAU TAO (SPINACH) NOODL

壽桃牌特級蝦子麵　　　壽桃牌特級菠菜

'COOK WITH YOUR SOUL, EAT WITH YOUR HEART'

# 4

# CHINESE
# CLASSICS

This chapter includes my very favourite recipe, which I've called 'Happiness in a Bowl'. It's a prawn wonton soup and is such a classic Chinese dish. You can rely on it, it's comforting and it won't let you down. It also won't have changed much over the last 2,000 years – that's the beauty of Chinese recipes. They don't evolve hugely, they remain traditional and they are full of flavour as well as being good for you. These Chinese classics are some of my favourites.

**For the fish stock**

a 3cm piece of fresh ginger,
cut in half and roughly bruised

1 stick of celery,
snapped in halves

shells and heads from
10 raw king prawns
(prawns used below)

**For the soup**

4 tinned water chestnuts,
drained and coarsely diced

4 tinned straw mushrooms,
drained and coarsely diced

10 raw king prawns, peeled
and roughly chopped

salt and ground white pepper

1 egg, separated

cornflour, to dust

8–10 wonton wrappers
(see page 23)

a handful of fresh thin
egg wonton noodles
(see page 23)

1 teaspoon sesame oil

1½–2 tablespoons oyster sauce

2 teaspoons light soy sauce

1 teaspoon fish sauce

2 spring onions, chopped

**To serve**

Chinese chilli oil
(see page 18)

When I think of warmth and happiness at the dinner table, I think of this bowl of beautiful food. Not only is it Poppa Wan's signature dish, it is also one of the most recognized Hong Kong – Chinese meals. I've cooked prawn wonton soup my whole life and yet I never get bored with it. Healthy, hearty and just downright gorgeous, this meal is like a best friend, favourite movie or the perfect man – steadfast, reliable and comforting.

1. Place the ginger, celery and prawn shells and heads into a saucepan. Cover with water and bring to the boil. Reduce the heat and simmer for up to 1 hour (10–15 minutes is fine). Drain the liquid through a sieve lined with muslin. Measure out 500ml of stock, topping up with boiled water, if needed.

2. Put the water chestnuts, straw mushrooms, prawns, a good pinch of salt and pepper and a third of the egg white in a large bowl. Mix well, squeezing the prawns between your fingers until you have chunks of sticky prawns rather than a runny mess.

3. Dust a work surface with cornflour and lay the wontons wrappers on top. Dust your hands with cornflour and pick up a wonton wrapper. Put a tablespoon of the prawn mixture in the centre of the wrapper and brush the edges with egg yolk. Bring the corners together over the middle of the mixture, then squeeze and twist the top to make a shape like a small sack. Repeat with the remaining mixture.

4. Boil a large pan of water. Separate the noodles and drop into the boiling water. Loosen the noodles using chopsticks and cook for 1–2 minutes. Once they are tender but still springy, remove them from the pan with a slotted spoon and run under a cold tap. Put them back into the pan of boiling water and cook for a further minute until warmed through, then remove and drain, adding sesame oil to keep the noodles from sticking together. Place the noodles into serving bowls and cover.

5. Put the drained stock into a saucepan and add the oyster sauce, soy sauce and fish sauce, along with a pinch of salt and pepper.

6. Sprinkle half of the spring onions over the cooked noodles in the serving bowls, add a little stock, then cover.

7. Drop the wontons into boiling water (you can use the water the noodles were cooked in) and cook for 6–8 minutes or until they float to the surface. They are cooked through when the wrapper is soft and the filling firm to touch. Remove and place on top of the noodles, then cover with the hot stock. Sprinkle with the remaining spring onions and serve with chilli oil on the side.

# 41. HAPPINESS IN A BOWL

PREPARATION TIME 25 MINUTES    COOKING TIME 30 MINUTES

**SERVES 2**

1 x 350g whole lemon sole

salt and ground white pepper

1–2 teaspoons light soy sauce

1–2 teaspoons fish sauce

a 3–4cm piece of fresh
ginger, peeled and cut
into matchsticks

½ a lemon, thinly sliced

**To serve**

1 tablespoon chopped
fresh chives

4 handfuls of rice
(a mixture of American long
grain and fragrant rice)

The Chinese community is one of the most social out there, and any excuse is used to get together. Because I'm always working I don't get the chance to cook for others as much as I used to, but maybe three times a year I'll spend two or three days putting a menu together, a day shopping and then I'll cook up a big banquet for my friends. Food means so much to me that I just want people to enjoy it. It's like a cleaver to my heart if they don't. This sole recipe is one I would serve up as part of a love-banquet for my nearest and dearest.

1. Place the sole on to a heatproof serving plate that fits into a deep, hob-proof roasting tray. Place two upturned ramekins into the roasting tray, then place the plate with the sole on top of them. Season both sides of the sole with salt and white pepper. Drizzle the soy and fish sauce over the sole and scatter over half of the ginger. Lay the slices of lemon over the fish, cutting them in half if necessary, then cover with the remaining ginger.

2. Carefully pour hot water into the roasting tray, making sure you don't get any on the plate containing the sole. Cover the roasting tray with foil, ensuring the foil doesn't touch the sole (make a tent if necessary) and place the tray directly on to the hob. Heat over a medium heat, ensuring that the water is simmering and steaming. Steam for 10–14 minutes or until the flesh is opaque.

3. Remove the plate from the roasting tray. Garnish the fish with chopped chives and serve with rice on the side (see below).

**FOR THE RICE**

1. Wash the rice, rubbing the grains together between your hands to release any excess starch. Change the water and repeat until the water is clear after rubbing.

2. Once you are ready to cook the rice, place it into a saucepan with a tight-fitting lid. Cover the rice with water so that the water comes 2cm above the level of the rice. Place the pan, without the lid, on to the hob and bring to the boil. Boil until the water has reduced and is forming bubbles at the top of the rice.

3. Cover and reduce the heat to the lowest setting and leave to cook for 10 minutes. Once all the water has been absorbed and the rice is tender, remove the lid, fluff the rice and leave to steam-dry a little before serving.

# 42. LEMON AND GINGER SOLE WITH MY FOOLPROOF RICE

PREPARATION TIME 5 MINUTES   COOKING TIME 14 MINUTES

16 dried shiitake mushrooms

salt and ground white pepper

2 tablespoons groundnut oil

3–4 cloves of garlic, peeled
and chopped

a 3cm piece of fresh ginger,
peeled and sliced

1½ medium onions, peeled
and sliced into thin wedges

300ml prawn-shell or fish
stock (see page 124)

1 tablespoon Shaoxing rice
wine or dry sherry

1–2 tablespoons oyster sauce

2 tablespoons dark soy sauce

1 tablespoon fish sauce

2 tablespoons light soy sauce

2 medium aubergines,
sliced into 6 long wedges and
stored in salted, cold water
until ready to use

1 teaspoon sesame oil

**For the beansprout salad**

2 handfuls of beansprouts

1 teaspoon sesame oil

1 tablespoon skinless peanuts,
roughly crushed

¼ of a fresh red chilli,
sliced diagonally

Many countries in Asia are predominately Buddhist, so vegetables often play the leading role when it comes to mealtime theatre. This dish is one of my personal favourites as it is beautifully tasty with an almost meat-like flavour. This is all down to the dried shiitake mushrooms that are sturdy in texture and deliciously salty. Couple them with the richness of fish sauce and the softness of aubergines, and this dish can be served to the most loyal of carnivores for a guaranteed result of happiness and amazement.

1. Soak the shiitake mushrooms in boiling water for 10 minutes, then drain and put half of the soaking liquor to one side.

2. Heat the oil in a wok over a medium-high heat and add the garlic and ginger. Stir-fry for 20 seconds, then add the onions and cook for 5 minutes until they begin to soften and colour on the edges, lowering the heat if necessary to prevent them burning. Season with salt and pepper and add the drained shiitake.

3. Gradually add 150ml of the fish stock, allowing it to reduce a little. Stir the vegetables, allowing them to absorb some of the stock. Add 4–5 tablespoons of the mushroom soaking liquor and then the Shaoxing rice wine, oyster sauce, dark soy sauce, fish sauce and light soy sauce. Taste and season with salt and pepper, adjusting the flavouring if necessary.

4. Drain the aubergine wedges and add to the wok, pushing them into the sauce. Add the rest of the fish stock, coating the aubergine in the sauce. Cover and leave to stew gently for 15–20 minutes or until the aubergine has softened but still holds its shape.

5. While the aubergine is stewing, soak the beansprouts in boiling water with some salt and pepper for 10 minutes, then drain. Drizzle over the sesame oil, season with a pinch of salt and pepper and mix in half of the crushed peanuts. Top with the chilli.

6. To serve, divide the aubergine and shiitake mix on to plates, drizzle with a little sesame oil and top with the sauce from the pan. Serve the beansprouts on the side in a mound with the remaining peanuts scattered on top.

PREPARATION TIME 10 MINUTES    COOKING TIME 30 MINUTES

# 43. AROMATIC AUBERGINE AND MUSHROOMS WITH BEANSPROUT SALAD

# 44. POPPA WAN'S EASY PEKING DUCK WITH PANCAKES

**SERVES 4**

1 tablespoon Chinese five-spice powder

1 whole duck (approx.1.5–2kg), gizzards and parsons nose removed

2 star anise

1 onion, peeled and roughly cut into wedges

a 5cm piece of fresh ginger, peeled and roughly sliced

4 cloves of garlic, peeled and bruised

2 spring onions, bruised

salt and ground white pepper

**To serve**

16 duck pancakes

1 cucumber, cut into matchsticks

5 spring onions, finely shredded

plum sauce (see page 135)

PREPARATION TIME
20 MINUTES

COOKING TIME
90 MINUTES

Growing up, Dad taught me and my siblings a couple of things that we've never forgotten. Firstly, the wisdom of the business: he taught us how to run a restaurant and work in the kitchens. Secondly, he taught us how to share food, because there is a real art to it. You need to make sure your guests are comfortable with the food they're eating, and that they have enough. Peking duck is a perfect sharing dish, and very well-known in the UK. I want to show you an easy, quick recipe, where the ducks are not deep-fried and you don't have to shred the meat. This is the way I like to cook traditional roast duck, accompanied by a homemade plum sauce – the whole dish is simple, and much tastier and healthier than the takeaway version you are used to.

1. Preheat your oven to 180°C/350°F/gas 4. Carefully sprinkle the five-spice powder into the cavity of the duck. It is important to try to cover as much of it as possible. Fill the cavity with the star anise, onion wedges, ginger, garlic and spring onions.

2. Using a 10cm skewer, secure the excess flap of neck skin at the head end of the duck. Next, pull together any excess skin around the main cavity and secure with a second skewer. This process will ensure that as much flavour as possible is kept within the duck.

3. Put the duck on to a rack over a deep roasting tray. Prick the skin all over with a fork, season with salt and place in the preheated oven. Roast the duck for 1 hour, then remove it from the oven. (It may be useful to remove as much of the fat from the bottom of the tray as you can at this point – it doesn't make a difference to the cooking, but it will save you a lot of cleaning later.)

4. Increase the temperature of the oven to 220°C/425°F/gas 7. Put the duck back into the oven and roast at the increased temperature for a further 25 minutes.

5. Take your duck out of the oven and leave it to rest for 15 minutes so that it is easier to handle. Remove the legs and the breast meat. Shred the leg meat and carve the breast meat.

6. Serve with steamed pancakes, cucumber, spring onions and plum sauce.

# 45. PERFECT PLUM SAUCE

**SERVES 8–10**

8 plums, stoned and chopped
roughly into 2cm pieces

1 teaspoon Chinese
five-spice powder

1 fresh red chilli, deseeded
and finely chopped

2–3 tablespoons runny honey

1 star anise

2–3 tablespoons light
soy sauce

2 tablespoons Shaoxing
rice wine or dry sherry

1–2 cloves of garlic, peeled
and finely chopped

1½ tablespoons dark
muscovado sugar

½ tablespoon ground
white pepper

1. Place the plums and 2 tablespoons of warm water in a large saucepan on a medium heat. Add the rest of the ingredients, using only 1 tablespoon of soy sauce and 2 tablespoons of honey to start with. Once the mixture has come to the boil, reduce the heat to a simmer.

2. Simmer the sauce until the plums are very tender, about 40 minutes depending on the ripeness of the fruit, stirring occasionally, until the plums are soft and collapsed. Taste and adjust the flavours as necessary. Do not let the mixture cook dry; add water if necessary.

3. Once the plums are tender, blend them with a stick blender until smooth. Taste and adjust the seasoning again with soy sauce and honey.

PREPARATION TIME 15 MINUTES
COOKING TIME 45 MINUTES

1 tablespoon groundnut oil

200g leftover duck meat, shredded

½ a cucumber, deseeded and cut into batons

2 spring onions, finely sliced into 4cm lengths

2 tablespoons hoisin sauce

150g dried fine egg noodles, cooked and drained according to the packet instructions

1 tablespoon light soy sauce (optional)

I hate waste. The best meals are sometimes, surprisingly, those using leftovers and the best thing about this type of cooking is that the more you experiment the more you will learn. It's taken me years and years of trying to perfect some leftover recipes but what's the worst that can happen if it goes wrong? You just try again. This stir-fry is a fantastic way of using up all the brilliant leftovers from Peking duck (see page 134) – enjoy it for lunch on your own the day after the dinner before . . .

1. Heat the oil in a wok over a high heat. When the oil is smoking, add the duck meat and stir-fry for 2–3 minutes, until the meat is beginning to turn golden and a little crisp.

2. Add the cucumber and spring onions and continue to stir-fry for 2 minutes, then add the hoisin sauce and a splash of water. Mix well.

3. Add the cooked noodles, with the soy sauce if using, and toss everything together. Serve immediately.

PREPARATION TIME 5 MINUTES    COOKING TIME 10 MINUTES

# 46. LEFTOVER ROAST DUCK NOODLES

**SERVES 4**

2 tablespoons groundnut oil

2 cloves of garlic, peeled
and finely sliced

300g choi sum (see page 20),
washed and cut to fit your wok

100ml water

2 tablespoons oyster sauce

1 tablespoon light soy sauce

1–2 teaspoons fish sauce

Once upon a wok, if you wanted to cook a fabulous Chinese vegetable dish then you'd need to haul yourself down to your local Chinatown to find the ingredients. But since the rise in popularity of Chinese cooking, major supermarkets now stock most of what's required, including beautiful leafy Asian vegetables. Choi sum is one of my favourites. The colour alone is delicious enough to make your eyes water with its emerald gleam. The thick, crunchy stalks are packed with flavour and the leaves boast enough health-giving properties to make a jar of vitamins blush. The simplicity of this dish is its virtue – toss the choi sum around a wok with some basic Chinese seasoning and you are left with a health-conscious and very tasty dish . . . yum!

1.  Heat the groundnut oil in a wok over a high heat. Once hot, add the garlic and stir-fry for 30 seconds.

2.  Add the choi sum and stir-fry for 2 minutes until the leaves begin to wilt. Pour in the water, being careful about spitting oil. Bring the water to the boil and cook on a high heat for a further 2 minutes, turning the choi sum a couple of times to ensure it's cooked evenly.

3.  Reduce the heat to medium and remove the choi sum to a serving plate, leaving as much of the residual liquid in the wok as possible. Quickly add the remaining ingredients, stirring well to incorporate, and turn the heat up to maximum, bringing the liquid to the boil.

4.  Pour the hot sauce over the cooked choi sum and serve immediately as part of a larger meal.

PREPARATION TIME 5 MINUTES    COOKING TIME 5 MINUTES

# 47. CHOI SUM IN OYSTER SAUCE

**MAKES 4 EGGS**

4 eggs at room temperature

150ml dark soy sauce

150ml light soy sauce

75ml Shaoxing rice wine
or dry sherry

**To serve**

½–1 fresh red chilli, deseeded
and finely chopped

1 tablespoon chopped
fresh chives

In some ways food means more to me than life itself. Not only has it been a way for me to communicate, a way for me to understand where my father is from and a way for my family to show me how much they love me, but food holds the key to the person I am. I vividly remember sitting cross-legged in front of the television, bathed and changed ready for bed, eating Grandma's eggs. I couldn't have been older than four or five, or taller than my grandfather's table. This dish may only contain a couple of eggs and a dash of soy sauce, but in its simplicity it holds the secrets of a true loving family: giving, sharing and appreciating. This recipe is my most treasured possession and I'd like to share it with you.

1. Bring a small pan of water to the boil. Carefully place the eggs in the water and boil for 4 minutes. As soon as they are cooked, drain the water, take the eggs out and run them under cold water until they are cool enough to handle (this also stops the cooking process).

2. Use a spoon to crack the eggs all over with delicate taps, then place them back in the pan and pour over the remaining ingredients. Top up with water so that the eggs are just covered. Bring the mixture back up to the boil and simmer for a further 10 minutes.

3. Once cooked, turn off the heat and leave the eggs to cool in the mixture for at least 20 minutes, preferably for a few hours.

4. When cool enough to handle, take out the eggs and peel them. You should find they have a beautifully mottled appearance.

5. Serve as part of a larger meal, or as a picnic snack. Lovely with a sprinkling of chopped red chilli and chives.

PREPARATION TIME 10 MINUTES     COOKING TIME 15 MINUTES

'FOOD IN THE HAND WILL WARM THE HEART'

# 5

## STREET FOOD: THE FAST AND THE FURIOUS

Street food is the Chinese version of snacking, but there is no junk food here! Visit any food market or night market in Hong Kong, China or elsewhere in Asia and you'll be treated to an awesome array of sights, sounds and smells as the hawkers cook up their wares. From fragrantly spiced noodles and marinated beancurd, to hot and crunchy spring rolls, this is food to enjoy on the move, warming you down to your soul.

**SERVES 4**

200g dried thin egg noodles

1 tablespoon groundnut oil

400g pork fillet or
tenderloin, cut into strips

a 2cm piece of fresh ginger,
peeled and roughly chopped

2 cloves of garlic, peeled and
roughly chopped

1 tablespoon shrimp paste

1 tablespoon soy sauce

1 tablespoon fish sauce

3 tablespoons water

salt and ground white pepper

1 carrot, peeled and cut into
matchsticks

2 spring onions, shredded

1 teaspoon sesame oil

There might seem to be a lot of cutting and chopping in this recipe, but once all your prep work is done, this dish will come together very quickly. I love the prep stage of any dish – it's the behind-the-scenes work that makes for a great cooking performance and is very satisfying.

1. Cook the noodles according to the packet instructions, then cool and set aside.

2. Heat the oil in a wok over a medium-high heat. Add the strips of pork and stir-fry for approximately 1 minute on each side, until the pork takes on some colour and is sealed but not quite cooked through. Remove from the wok, and set aside.

3. Turn the heat up to high. Add the ginger and garlic and stir-fry for 20 seconds until softened a little. Add the ground dried shrimp and continue to stir-fry until aromatic. Add the soy sauce, fish sauce and the water and cook for 10 seconds.

4. Check the noodles. Once softened, but retaining a slight bite, drain. Add the noodles and the pork strips to the wok, tossing them well through the wok for 1 minute to warm and coat in the sauce. Season with salt and pepper if needed.

5. Remove to a serving plate and garnish with the raw carrot and spring onions. Sprinkle over a couple of drops of sesame oil and serve.

PREPARATION TIME 10 MINUTES    COOKING TIME 10 MINUTES

# 49. SUPER SPEEDY NOODLES WITH PORK AND GINGER

**SERVES 2–4**

4 boneless chicken thighs,
skin removed

4 raw king prawns, de-veined
and peeled, but tails
still attached

a 3cm piece of
fresh ginger, bruised

3 cloves of garlic,
halved and bruised

4 spring onions,
halved and bruised

½ a fresh red chilli,
finely chopped

1–2 tablespoons fish sauce

1–2 tablespoons light
soy sauce

1 tablespoon Shaoxing
rice wine or dry sherry

½–1 tablespoon
sesame oil, to taste

½–1 tablespoon
groundnut oil

salt and ground white pepper

**For the sauce**

2 tablespoons fish sauce

2 tablespoons light soy sauce

2 tablespoons Shaoxing rice
wine or dry sherry

1 tablespoon dark soy sauce

4 tablespoons runny honey

¼ of a fresh red chilli,
deseeded and chopped

lemon wedges, to serve

Some people remember football games, school trips or favourite songs when they think about their earliest memories. I don't! Mealtimes have always been the main link to my childhood: tables overflowing with delicious food, pack-ups prepared by Momma Wan filled with Chinese surprises, or distinctive flavours that signified a celebration. This dish of deep-fried, paper-bagged chicken and prawns is so embedded in my memories, even the idea of eating it now makes me feel like I'm ten years old again. Dad would prepare this in the restaurant at Chinese New Year. Our customers would 'oooh' and 'ahhh' as we placed plates full of wrapped-up presents in front of them as if it was Christmas morning. It was wonderful to watch them unwrap the parcels, which looked just like the picture opposite. My version of this very special dish has been baked in the oven – much easier to achieve at home, and much healthier too.

1. Mix the chicken, prawns, ginger, garlic, spring onions, chilli, fish sauce, soy sauce, Shaoxing rice wine and groundnut and sesame oils in a bowl or large freezer bag. Season with salt and pepper, mix well to ensure that the chicken and prawns are covered in the marinade, and put in the fridge to marinate for 45 minutes.

2. When you are ready to cook, preheat the oven to 200°C/400°/gas 6. Cut 4 rectangles of baking or parchment paper so that each piece is just larger than a sheet of A4 paper. Place 1 prawn and a couple of pieces of spring onion inside each chicken thigh, and wrap the thigh around the prawn. Season with salt and pepper and draw the sides of the paper up. Add a spoonful of marinade to each parcel and then fold the sides over on each other, rolling the edges together and seal by stapling or using paperclips. Place the parcels on an oven tray and bake for 15 minutes.

3. Pour any remaining marinade into a wok over a medium heat. Add the ingredients for the sauce, omitting the chilli, and bring to a simmer, stirring to melt the honey. Add the chilli to taste. When the sauce has thickened enough to coat the back of a spoon, remove and pour into a small bowl to serve.

4. Remove the baking tray from the oven and serve the parcels for your guests to open themselves, with the sauce to pour over.

# 50. SPICY CHICKEN AND PRAWN PARCELS

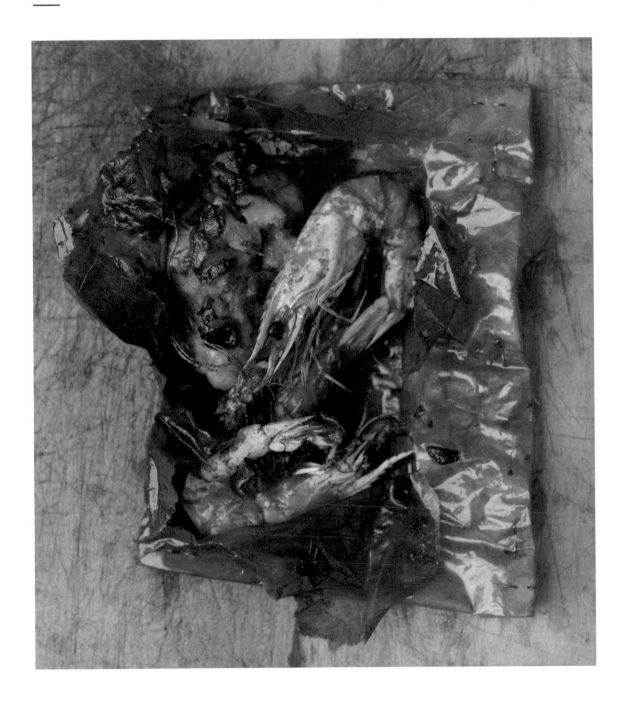

PREPARATION TIME 60 MINUTES    COOKING TIME 15 MINUTES

**SERVES 2**

2 tablespoons groundnut oil

2 cloves of garlic,
peeled and bruised

a 2cm piece of fresh ginger,
peeled and sliced

3 spring onions, trimmed,
halved and bruised

250g stewing beef,
preferably flank or shin,
cut into 3cm cubes

1 star anise

½ teaspoon Chinese
five-spice powder

½ a cinnamon stick

1 litre beef stock

3–4 tablespoons Shaoxing
rice wine or dry sherry

2 tablespoons light soy sauce

2 teaspoons fish sauce

1 tablespoon oyster sauce

200g precooked ho fun
noodles (see page 21)

4 leaves of Chinese
cabbage, shredded

1 spring onion, finely sliced

Forget the multi-dish platters, considered assortments or the requirement to share . . . sometimes all you want is a one-pot meal. Over hundreds of years, the Chinese have developed the art of noodle-making. Whether it's thin *al dente* wonton noodles, thick and starchy ho fun or carefully hand-crafted dragon noodles, there seems to be a noodle for every mood and occasion. This dish is beautifully fragrant with five-spice and, considering the amount of flavour, healthy beyond belief. Surely nothing that tastes this good can be so healthy! Prepare, cook, devour – it's that simple.

1. Heat the oil in a saucepan over a high heat. When hot, add the ginger, garlic, halved spring onions and the beef and fry until the meat is golden on all sides.

2. Add the star anise, five-spice powder, cinnamon and beef stock, and bring to a simmer. Add the Shaoxing rice wine, taste and season with salt and pepper if necessary. Simmer for 1–2 hours, until the meat is tender. Top up the liquid level with water if needed.

3. Once the beef is tender, strain the liquid into a clean pan. Discard the whole spices and the chunks of ginger and garlic and put the meat to one side. Heat the liquid through, adding the soy sauce, fish sauce and oyster sauce when the stock is hot. Taste and add more water if the flavour is too intense.

4. Bring a pan of water to the boil and blanch the noodles for 2–3 minutes, stirring to separate and soften, then strain. Divide the noodles between the serving bowls and add the cabbage to each bowl.

5. Divide the beef between the bowls and pour over the hot soup. Sprinkle over the sliced spring onions and serve.

PREPARATION TIME 10 MINUTES    COOKING TIME 1–2 HOURS

# 51. POPPA WAN'S ALL-TIME FAVOURITE BEEF NOODLE SOUP

2 tablespoons groundnut oil

2 large cloves of garlic, peeled and finely sliced

a 3cm piece of fresh ginger, peeled and finely sliced

2 spring onions, trimmed, halved and bruised

250g morning glory (see page 21), cut into 4cm pieces

½ a fresh red chilli, deseeded and finely sliced

3–4 tablespoons hot water

1 tablespoon Shaoxing rice wine or dry sherry

1 tablespoon light soy sauce

2 teaspoons fish sauce

1 tablespoon rice wine vinegar

1 teaspoon caster sugar (optional)

200g firm tofu, drained and cut into 2cm dice

salt and ground white pepper sesame oil, to taste

For me, there are many similarities between a beautiful outfit and a fabulous meal. Both are complete works of art and both are most definitely at the heart of my passion for life. Like any wonderful outfit, however, if you get your accessories wrong you could destroy the whole look; the same rules apply to a carefully crafted menu. Think of this recipe as the perfect shoes. Simple and elegant, you know you can always rely on it to jazz up a meal without upstaging the main dish. The beauty of this is there are so many different ways to serve it: 'dress it up' with an eye-watering dollop of Malaysian sambal or 'dress it down' by leaving out the tofu, keeping it casual and somewhat capsule. Either way, when this dish arrives on my family's table we know we are in for a home-cooked couturier climax!

1. Heat the oil in a wok over a medium to high heat. When hot, add the garlic, ginger and spring onions and stir-fry for 30 seconds until the spring onions turn slightly golden and have softened.

2. Add the morning glory and the chilli and stir well, then add the hot water to steam the morning glory. Once the water has slightly reduced, pour in the Shaoxing rice wine, soy sauce, fish sauce, caster sugar and vinegar. Reduce the heat to medium and stir to combine.

3. Make a well in the middle of the wok by pushing all the ingredients to the sides. Carefully place the pieces of tofu in the space you have created. Put a lid on the wok and let the whole dish steam for 3 minutes. Remove the lid and very carefully mix all the ingredients together.

4. Taste, adjust the seasoning with salt and white pepper if necessary, put on the serving dish and sprinkle over a few drops of sesame oil before serving.

PREPARATION TIME 10 MINUTES    COOKING TIME 5 MINUTES

## 52. **STIR-FRIED MORNING GLORY WITH SILKY TOFU**

**SERVES 2–4**

3 tablespoons smooth
peanut butter

2 tablespoons fish sauce

2 tablespoons light soy sauce

1 tablespoon groundnut oil

2 teaspoons sesame oil

salt and ground white pepper

half a boned lamb shoulder,
(approx 500g), cut into
2.5cm cubes

1 medium cucumber,
halved, deseeded and
cut into 2.5cm chunks

**For the cabbage salad**

¼ of a Chinese leaf cabbage,
shredded

½ a carrot, peeled and cut
into matchsticks

3 spring onions (green parts
only), trimmed and shredded

juice of ½ a lemon

**To serve**

2 tablespoons toasted
peanuts, chopped

As with making dumplings, putting together these little skewers of loveliness with your kids is a great thing to do because you can get them involved – if you spear the meat on to the skewers, you can let them have a go at carefully putting the pieces of cucumber on. A ready-prepared plate of these in your fridge is a great alternative to a bag of chips or a kebab after a night at the pub.

1. Mix together the peanut butter, fish sauce and soy sauce, sesame and groundnut oils. Taste and adjust the seasoning with salt and pepper, then add the lamb pieces. Stir the lamb around in the marinade to mix well, making sure it is coated on all sides. Marinate the lamb in the mix for at least 1 hour, or ideally overnight.

2. Once ready to cook, mix together the cabbage, carrot, spring onions and lemon juice to make the salad. Taste and season with salt and pepper if necessary, then set aside.

3. Heat a griddle pan until hot. Thread the cubes of meat and the cucumber in turns on to skewers. Brush with a little oil if the marinade seems too dry, then place on the griddle pan to cook on all sides, turning now and again so that they are evenly coloured and a little charred, until just cooked through (about 8–10 minutes).

4. Remove the skewers from the pan, and garnish with a sprinkling of chopped, toasted peanuts before serving.

PREPARATION TIME 1 HOUR 10 MINUTES    COOKING TIME 10 MINUTES

## 53. GRIDDLED LAMB AND CUCUMBER SKEWERS WITH FRESH CABBAGE SALAD

**SERVES 2**

1 tablespoon groundnut oil

2 lap chong/Chinese sausages
(see page 18), sliced diagonally

2 large tubes of squid, cleaned

½ teaspoon dried chilli flakes

lemon juice

salt and ground white pepper,
to taste

**To serve**

2 tablespoons chopped fresh
parsley or 1 spring onion, sliced

Lap chong is delicious – a smoky-sweet cured sausage, it's the Chinese equivalent to Spanish chorizo and is fantastic when paired with squid. This dish shows both ingredients off to the max.

1. Place the lap chong and the oil in a cold wok. Turn the heat on to a low setting, and allow the fat to gently render from the sausage as you prepare the squid.

2. With the narrow point of one of the squid tubes facing you, slice it lengthways to create two long halves of squid. Place one half to the side as you concentrate your efforts on one piece at a time. With the inside of the squid facing out, slash the flesh, (being careful not to cut all the way through) on a 45° angle at intervals of about 5mm. Once you have done this turn the squid through 90° and repeat the process to create a criss-cross pattern. Once the pattern has been created slice the squid all the way through at 2cm intervals so that you end up with criss-crossed ribbons. Place in a bowl and repeat with the remaining squid. Dry the squid thoroughly on kitchen paper.

3. By the time you have prepared your squid the sausage should have rendered out a lot of deliciously flavoured oil and the outside should have turned crisp. With a slotted spoon, remove the sausage from the wok and set aside.

4. Turn up the heat to high, and stir-fry the squid for 2–3 minutes, until it turns golden and curls up at the edges. Add the sausage back into the wok and reduce the heat to medium before sprinkling in the chilli flakes and stir-frying for 1 minute.

5. Remove from the heat, add a generous squeeze of lemon, season with salt and pepper and garnish with chopped parsley or spring onion.

PREPARATION TIME 15 MINUTES    COOKING TIME 10 MINUTES

**SERVES 2**

2 tablespoons groundnut oil

1 small onion, peeled and
finely sliced

1 clove of garlic, peeled
and finely chopped

1 teaspoon hot curry powder

2 eggs, beaten

100g char siu pork, cut
into bite-size pieces

150g mixed seafood, cooked

3 tablespoons peas,
fresh or frozen

1 small carrot, peeled
and cut into matchsticks

salt and ground white pepper

150g vermicelli or egg
noodles, soaked and
drained according to packet
instructions (see page 22)

light soy sauce, to taste

**To garnish**

2 spring onions, shredded

One of my favourite places to eat in the world is Singapore. I just love the hawker markets – huge open-air food centres filled to the brim with every flavour of Asia. There's nothing you can't find in a hawker market and quite often you'll get a few surprises along the way too. Everywhere you look you are teased and flirted with by fabulous dishes from around the continent. Bowls of herbal Chinese soup, fat white Vietnamese spring rolls, Hong Kong's finest baskets of dim sum or perfectly skewered Malaysian *rojak*, a delicious fruit and vegetable salad served with cucumber and rice patties. Singapore noodles is like your very own hawker market on a plate, with char siu pork borrowed from Hong Kong, curry powder on loan from India and vermicelli noodles nicked from China. This dish really is the emperor of fusion cooking.

1. Heat a wok over a medium to high heat and add the oil. Add the onion and stir-fry until tender and beginning to colour at the edges. Add the garlic and curry powder and cook for 30 seconds, or until aromatic.

2. Push the onion and garlic to one side of the wok, then add the beaten eggs and cook over a medium heat, scrambling the eggs until cooked through and coloured round the edges.

3. Add the pork and stir-fry to heat it through. Add the mixed seafood and heat through.

4. Add the peas and carrots and stir-fry over a medium-high heat until the peas are cooked. Season with salt and pepper.

5. Add the noodles to the wok, adding another dash of oil if necessary. Stir-fry over a high heat, coating the noodles in the curry-flavoured oil at the bottom of the wok and gently mixing them with the other ingredients.

6. Season with a dash of soy sauce if needed, and serve garnished with the shredded spring onions.

PREPARATION TIME 10 MINUTES    COOKING TIME 15 MINUTES

# 55. DAD'S SINGAPORE NOODLES

**For the salad**

350g cooked chicken, torn into strips

250g vermicelli noodles, soaked and drained according to packet instructions (see page 22)

I medium cucumber, roughly peeled, sliced lengthways, deseeded and finely sliced

2 carrots, peeled and cut into matchsticks

I fennel bulb, very finely sliced

2 spring onions, cut into matchsticks

a small bunch of fresh mint, leaves roughly torn

salt and ground white pepper

**For the dressing**

4 tablespoons freshly squeezed lime juice

I–2 teaspoons fish sauce, to taste

a pinch of caster sugar

½ a fresh long red chilli, finely chopped

½ teaspoon sesame oil

Whether it's catering for a dinner party, birthday party, wedding or the biggest celebration in Asia, Chinese New Year, the look and aesthetic of the food we serve is hugely important. The Chinese have a brilliant knack of paring down even the most complicated of dishes, simply serving them on a three-way palette of black, gold and red. When dressing your delicious food to serve to friends and family, adopt as your mantra Coco Chanel's formidable quote: 'When accessorizing always take off the last thing you put on.' If you employ this simple technique to your food, I guarantee it will look as gorgeous as it tastes fabulous. This dish is so versatile, it works both hot and cold.

1. Make the dressing by mixing all the ingredients together. Taste and adjust as necessary so that you have a harmonious balance of flavours, with none more dominant than the others.

2. Put the salad ingredients into a bowl and mix together, tossing the noodles around to separate the strands and combine them well with the other ingredients. Pour over a little of the dressing and toss. Season with a pinch of salt and pepper if necessary.

3. Put the salad into a serving dish and pour over the remaining dressing, mixing well to coat the noodles.

PREPARATION TIME 5 MINUTES

# 56. VIETNAMESE STYLE LEFTOVER CHICKEN SALAD

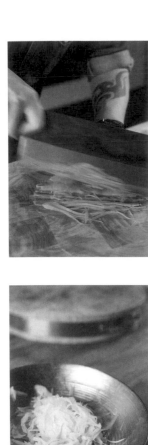

**For the pork filling**

1 tablespoon groundnut oil

2 cloves of garlic, peeled and finely chopped

a 2cm piece of fresh ginger, peeled and finely chopped

200g minced pork

½ tablespoon fish sauce

a pinch of caster sugar

1 tablespoon rice vinegar

salt and ground white pepper

**For the dipping sauce**

1 tablespoon caster sugar

juice of 2 limes

2 fresh red chillies, deseeded and chopped

2 cloves of garlic, peeled and chopped

5 tablespoons water

½ tablespoon rice vinegar

2 tablespoons fish sauce

**For the rolls**

12 round rice paper sheets (16cm diameter)

2 tablespoons fresh mint leaves, 12 whole leaves, remainder torn

a bunch of fresh coriander, leaves torn

1 large carrot, cut into matchsticks

2–3 spring onions, shredded

a handful of beansprouts, rinsed

¼ of an iceberg lettuce, shredded

200g cooked vermicelli noodles (see page 22)

juice of 2 limes

fish sauce, to taste

I've been brought up on a diet of strong flavours. When I was younger, my mum served me and my brother and sister some homemade chips and we all cried because we didn't like them! To our palates they were too bland and had no flavour. My mum is the most incredible cook of Chinese food – she's learned over the years from my dad. One thing we do enjoy eating in our family are spring and summer rolls. Spring rolls are fried and crispy, summer rolls are soft and light. These Vietnamese rolls taste like summer to me because of their filling – minced pork with little bursts of mint in each mouthful. Bland chips vs summer rolls? No contest.

1. Heat a wok over a medium heat and add the groundnut oil. Add the garlic and ginger and fry until softened, then add the pork and stir-fry until browned slightly and cooked through.

2. Add the fish sauce, sugar, vinegar and a little salt and pepper and stir to combine. Cook for a minute or two, until the mince has had a chance to absorb the flavours of the sauce and the sauce is coating the mince. Set aside to cool.

3. To make the dipping sauce, put the sugar and lime juice into a bowl and stir until the sugar has dissolved. Add the remaining ingredients, mix, taste and adjust as necessary. Set aside.

4. Dip the rice paper sheets briefly into a bowl of warm water, until softened slightly, then wrap in a clean damp cloth. Mix the torn mint leaves with the coriander leaves. Put the remaining ingredients in a row, ready to stuff the rolls.

5. Lay a soaked rice paper sheet flat on a clean surface and place a tablespoon of mixed herbs in the middle. Add a couple of pieces of carrot and spring onion, a few beansprouts and a tablespoon of shredded lettuce. Top with a tablespoon of noodles, and add a little lime juice and a drop of fish sauce. Add a tablespoon of the pork mince mixture. Fold over two sides of the rice paper to enclose the filling and roll over once, then slowly roll once again, tucking the edges of the rice paper into the middle as you go. When the roll is complete, seal it by lightly brushing the edge with warm water.

6. Repeat the process with the remaining ingredients, or let your guests assemble the rolls themselves. If making the rolls in advance, cover them with clingfilm to prevent them drying out.

7. Serve the rolls with the dipping sauce.

# 57. VIETNAMESE STYLE SUMMER ROLLS FILLED WITH PORK

# 58. SPRING ROLLS

**SERVES 4**

vegetable oil, for deep frying

50g firm tofu, minced into small pieces with the back of a fork

2 spring onions, very finely sliced into small rounds

1 small carrot, peeled and coarsely grated

25g beansprouts

½ a daikon, peeled and cut into matchsticks

2 water chestnuts, chopped very finely

a 1cm piece of fresh ginger, peeled and very finely diced

2 tablespoons oyster sauce

1 tablespoon light soy sauce

2 teaspoons fish sauce

salt and ground white pepper

4 large, square spring roll wrappers, each cut into 4 small squares (see page 22)

a little water, to seal

As a child I got teased for being mixed race – I was very slightly different to my peers. For years I couldn't understand where those differences came from – was it because I was a bit fatter, a bit taller or a bit camper than other boys around me? The answer's no. My difference was expressed through food. Most kids, when hungry for a snack, reach for a salty packet of crisps or a generic chocolate bar, but I reached for something a little more unusual. When I was teased for snacking on a delicious spring roll, whilst it might have hurt on the surface, I knew I was loved and warm on the inside.

1. Preheat your oil to 180°C. If you don't have a heatproof thermometer then you know the oil is ready when a cube of bread dropped into the oil turns golden in about 10 seconds.

2. Thoroughly mix together all the remaining ingredients apart from the spring roll wrappers and the water.

3. Place one of the quartered wrappers diagonally on to a clean surface. Place a sixteenth of the mixture in a small horizontal line across the centre of the wrapper, leaving a 1cm border on each side. Dip your finger in some water and run it around the border of the wrapper.

4. Pull the bottom corner of the wrapper up and over the mixture, followed by each side. Roll the pastry, tucking the mixture in tightly until you reach the end. Press lightly to ensure the end has stuck properly. Put to one side on a dry chopping board and repeat with the remaining mixture and wrappers.

5. Once all your spring rolls are complete, fry them in batches of 4 to avoid the oil boiling over. Drop each batch carefully into the hot oil and deep-fry for 2–3 minutes or until they have turned a lovely golden colour.

6. Serve immediately with a little sweet chilli sauce as part of a larger meal.

PREPARATION TIME 15–20 MINUTES    COOKING TIME 3–4 MINUTES

300g dried thin egg noodles

2 teaspoons sesame oil

1 litre fresh chicken stock

1 tablespoon Chinese chilli oil
(see page 18)

2 tablespoons groundnut oil

200g minced pork

1 teaspoon Sichuan
peppercorns

4 spring onions, trimmed and
finely sliced

200g Chinese preserved
mustard greens,
drained and sliced

2 tablespoons Shaoxing rice
wine or dry sherry

2 tablespoons light soy sauce

2 tablespoons rice vinegar

If there's one dish that's going to blow away the cobwebs then it's my quick Dan Dan noodles. If you have a cold, are generally bunged up, or just need a kick-start to your day then reach for the chilli oil and peppercorns. The broth is best made with fresh chicken stock, but can be substituted for a cube if you are desperate for a chilli fix.

1. Cook the noodles according to the packet instructions, then drain and set aside. When cool, toss the sesame oil through the noodles.

2. Pour the stock into a large saucepan over a high heat. Bring to the boil, then reduce the heat so the stock is simmering and add the chilli oil. Reduce the heat to low, to keep the stock warm whilst you prepare the other ingredients.

3. Heat the oil in a wok over a high heat. Add the minced pork and stir-fry for 2–3 minutes until cooked through and turning brown. Reduce the heat and add the Sichuan peppercorns and half of the sliced spring onions. Stir-fry for a further minute.

4. Once the spring onions have softened a little and the peppercorns have changed colour to a darker red, add the drained mustard greens and stir to incorporate. Stir-fry for a further 2 minutes.

5. Pour in the Shaoxing rice wine, soy sauce and the vinegar. Stir well then cook over a medium heat for 2 minutes until the liquid has reduced.

6. Divide the noodles between the serving bowls, then spoon the pork and greens mixture on top, before pouring over enough stock to almost cover.

7. Garnish with the remaining spring onions before slurping down greedily.

PREPARATION TIME 25 MINUTES MINIMUM
COOKING TIME 8–10 MINUTES

**SERVES 1–2**

225g plain flour, plus extra for dusting

salt and ground white pepper

2 tablespoons groundnut oil, or 30g lard, melted, plus extra for shallow frying

**For the filling**

200g minced pork

4 raw king prawns, peeled, de-veined and chopped

5 small red radishes, trimmed and chopped

a 2cm piece of fresh ginger, peeled and finely chopped

2 tablespoons chopped fresh chives

1 teaspoon light soy sauce

1 small clove of garlic, peeled and finely chopped

**For the dipping sauce**

2 tablespoons light soy sauce

2 teaspoons rice vinegar

1 tablespoon sweet chilli sauce, or 1 teaspoon chilli sauce of your choice

juice of ¼ of a lime

This may seem an odd pairing of ingredients, but it works beautifully. I love the way the pink and white hues of the radish combine so well with the deep savoury brown of seasoned pork mince. Don't be fooled into thinking that the radish is there purely to look pretty; it provides a mature, peppery note that adds a touch of class to this street-food classic.

1. Put the flour and a pinch of salt and pepper into a large bowl. Make a well in the centre and pour in the oil or lard and 100ml of hot water, then mix to form a dough, adding a little more water if it isn't quite coming together.

2. Knead the dough on a floured work surface for a couple of minutes, until smooth and elastic. Place in a clean bowl, cover and leave to rest while you make the filling – alternatively you can leave the dough for a couple of hours before using, if you prefer.

3. Place the filling ingredients in a bowl, combine and season.

4. Once you're ready to assemble your pancakes, place the dough on a floured work surface and cut it into 4 pieces. Flatten each piece into a disc about 1cm thick, either with a rolling pin or the palm of your hand.

5. Divide the filling into 4 and place a portion in the centre of each disc, patting it down a little. Gently pull the edges of the dough outwards and fold over the mixture. To create a tidy fold, start at the top, then the bottom, then the sides until you have covered the filling completely with dough and the pancake is round. Pinch the middle where the edges join, to seal the pancake, and smooth with your fingers. The pancake buns should be about 10cm in diameter and 2.5cm thick – if not, flatten them a little with the palm of your hand.

6. Heat 3cm of oil in a large, high-sided frying pan. Heat the oil to 180°C (if you don't have a heatproof thermometer then you know the oil is ready when a cube of bread dropped into the oil turns golden in about 10 seconds). Add the buns, join side down. Shallow fry for 7–10 minutes, turning once. When ready, remove on to kitchen paper to absorb any axcess oil.

7. Flip the pancakes over and cook on the other side for 3–4 minutes, or until golden and crisp. Once cooked through and golden, drain well on kitchen paper.

8. Meanwhile make the dipping sauce: mix together the ingredients, tasting and adjusting the seasoning as necessary.

9. Serve the pancakes warm, with the dipping sauce alongside.

# 60. PORK AND RADISH PANCAKE BUNS

PREPARATION TIME 25 MINUTES   COOKING TIME 10 MINUTES

'FOOD WITH FAMILY AND FRIENDS IS ALWAYS A CELEBRATION'

# 6

# FEASTING

The most giving thing you can do for someone is to feed them. I take my cooking quite
seriously and I think I cried once when a
dinner I made for others didn't turn out
exactly right! Dad always taught us to
give 100 per cent no matter what we were
doing, and I like to give 100 per cent to my
cooking and to my guests. The dishes in
this section are all fantastic for serving up
to a group of friends or family, especially
for a celebration. But don't cry if something
goes a little wrong – experience will help
you to improve. I now think that if it looks a
bit rubbish but tastes amazing, who cares?

2 tablespoons groundnut oil

a 3cm piece of fresh ginger,
peeled and chopped

4 cloves of garlic,
peeled and chopped

500g chicken breast or
boneless thigh meat,
minced or finely chopped

¼ of a red pepper, deseeded
and finely chopped

6 water chestnuts, drained
and chopped

100g tinned bamboo shoots,
drained and chopped

8 tinned straw mushrooms,
drained and chopped

1 tablespoon Shaoxing
rice wine or dry sherry

1 tablespoon light soy sauce

2 teaspoons dark soy sauce

1 tablespoon fish sauce

salt and ground white pepper

1 tablespoon cashew nuts,
finely chopped

### To serve

2–3 baby gem lettuces,
leaves separated

2 tomatoes, deseeded
and finely diced

½ a cucumber, finely diced

sesame oil, to taste

I cannot remember a single childhood meal that didn't revolve around sharing with my family – not just the food that Mum and Dad had prepared and placed at the centre of the table but also the stories from our day, gossip about the family and, of course, the love we had for one another. Sharing and giving is truly what Chinese food is about and this recipe demonstrates that perfectly. An enormous plate of stir-fried garlicky chicken, steaming hot and full of simple flavours, waiting to be wrapped adoringly into crispy lettuce leaves and then either passed to one another or unashamedly devoured until the entire plateful has vanished. Forget diamonds and fast cars, this is what life is about – giving, sharing and enjoying with the ones we care about most.

1. Heat 1 tablespoon of oil in a wok over a medium heat. Once hot, add the ginger and garlic and fry until softened. Add the chicken and stir-fry over a medium heat until browned slightly and cooked through. Remove the chicken and set to one side.

2. Clean out the wok, then place back on the heat, adding the rest of the oil. Add the red pepper, cook for 30 seconds, then stir in the water chestnuts, bamboo shoots and straw mushrooms, and cook for 30 seconds more. Add the chicken back into the wok.

3. Add the Shaoxing rice wine, soy sauce, fish sauce and a little salt and pepper. Mix well and cook for a minute or two until the chicken has absorbed the flavours of the sauce and the sauce has reduced a little. Add the cashew nuts and mix well.

4. To serve, fill the lettuce leaves with a little of the chicken mixture and place them on a serving plate. Scatter over the diced tomato and cucumber and add a few drops of sesame oil. Serve immediately.

PREPARATION TIME 10 MINUTES
COOKING TIME 10 MINUTES

# 61. FRAGRANT CHINESE CHICKEN WRAPPED IN LETTUCE LEAVES

1 x 1kg fresh lobster
(ask your fishmonger
to kill it for you)

1 tablespoon groundnut oil

4 cloves of garlic, peeled,
2 finely chopped, 2 bruised

a 6cm piece of fresh ginger,
peeled (half sliced,
half bruised)

8 spring onions, trimmed,
halved and bruised

1½ tablespoons Shaoxing
rice wine or dry sherry

2 tablespoons light soy sauce

1 tablespoon oyster sauce

½ tablespoon fish sauce

150ml chicken, fish or
vegetable stock

salt and ground white pepper

300g vermicelli noodles,
soaked and drained according
to packet instructions
(see page 22)

If you're the kind of person who cleans before your cleaner arrives then you will totally understand what I'm about to say. A dirty kitchen is something that should never happen to good people. I'm unsure whether my kitchen OCD is a result of my years of training in a restaurant, where hygiene and cleanliness absolutely comes before anything else, or whether it's because I'm a control freak. Either way, cooking etiquette for me revolves around wiping, cleaning, throwing away and maintaining an angelically clear work surface. As far as I'm concerned, OCD stands for Only Cooking Delicious. Particularly when it comes to making this dish.

1. Place the lobster into a bamboo steamer over salted boiling water. Steam for 18 minutes.

2. Meanwhile, heat the oil in a wok over a medium heat. When hot, add the garlic and ginger and stir-fry until the ginger has softened a little. Add the spring onions and stir-fry until wilted. Add the Shaoxing rice wine, soy sauce, oyster sauce and fish sauce, and cook for 30 seconds. Add the stock, stir well and bring to the boil, heating for 4–5 minutes to reduce a little. Taste, and season with salt and pepper if necessary.

3. Once the lobster is cooked, remove from the steamer and place on a chopping board. Remove the claws and legs by twisting them at their base. Separate the head from the tail and slice the tail into chunks along the joints, leaving the meat in the shell.

4. Crack the claws by hitting them with the handle or broad part of a heavy knife, so that it is easier to get at the meat when serving. Cut the head in half and remove the sand sack from the lobster head.

5. Add the softened noodles to the pan with the sauce and toss for 30 seconds to warm through. Add the lobster pieces and gently turn in the pan to mix and flavour the noodles, tossing and scraping the wok as you go.

6. Remove from the heat and serve, arranging the pieces of lobster on top of the noodles.

PREPARATION TIME 30 MINUTES    COOKING TIME 25 MINUTES

# 62. LUXURIOUS LOBSTER NOODLES

**SERVES 4**

500ml Shaoxing rice wine
or dry sherry

2 star anise

a 5cm piece of fresh ginger,
peeled and bruised

3 cloves of garlic,
peeled and bruised

3 spring onions,
finely chopped

3 tablespoons light soy sauce

1.25kg piece of pork belly,
rind left on but unscored

**For the glaze**

4 tablespoons runny honey

2 tablespoons light soy sauce

**To garnish**

1 fresh red chilli, deseeded
and sliced diagonally

2 spring onions,
sliced diagonally

What can I say about this, other than that it's quite simply one of the best things you will ever put in your mouth! I promise.

1. Place the Shaoxing rice wine, star anise, ginger, garlic, spring onions and soy sauce into a large pan. Add the pork belly and pour over enough water to generously cover the meat. Bring to the boil over a high heat, then reduce the heat and simmer for 1½–2 hours, or until the pork is very tender, turning occasionally to ensure even cooking. Leave the pork in its cooking liquid until cool enough to handle.

2. Preheat your oven to 200°C/400°F/gas 6. Remove the pork from the liquid and place it on a board. Using a knife, carefully remove the very top layer of skin. Line a flat baking tray with baking parchment to protect your tray, and place the pork on the lined tray.

3. Mix together the honey and soy sauce and pour the mixture over the pork. It will run down and off the pork, but don't worry about it. Place the pork in the oven and roast for 20–30 minutes, turning often and basting with the glaze to achieve a glossy lacquered look.

4. Remove from the oven and place on a serving plate. Slice the pork into large chunks and garnish with the spring onion and chilli.

PREPARATION TIME 10 MINUTES    COOKING TIME 2–3 HOURS

# 63. POPPA WAN'S SHOW-STOPPING TWICE-COOKED MELTING PORK

4 dried shiitake mushrooms

2 tablespoons groundnut oil

a 2cm piece of fresh ginger,
peeled and finely chopped

2 cloves of garlic, peeled
and finely chopped

5 spring onions,
finely shredded

500g assorted fresh
mushrooms (such as chestnut,
enoki and oyster), cleaned
and sliced or separated

2 tablespoons Shaoxing
rice wine or dry sherry

2 tablespoons light soy sauce

1 tablespoon fish sauce

1 tablespoon oyster sauce

ground white pepper

**To garnish**

1 teaspoon sesame oil

1 spring onion, shredded

½ a fresh red chilli, deseeded
and thinly sliced

Mushrooms are full of flavour and are really important in Chinese cooking. There are so many types available in the supermarkets now, so decide to experiment. This simple dish can be whacked in the wok and will literally be ready in moments. Serve with some rice and you have a great veggie meal on its own, or have as a side dish to a more showy main course.

1. Put the dried shiitake mushrooms into a bowl and pour boiling water over them. Leave them to stand for a minimum of 5 minutes. Remove the mushrooms from the water and squeeze out any excess water, retaining the liquid in the bowl.

2. Heat the oil in a wok over a high heat. Once hot, add the ginger, garlic and spring onions. Stir-fry for 30 seconds, then add the drained dried shiitake mushrooms and stir-fry for 1 minute.

3. Add the assorted fresh mushrooms to the wok and stir-fry for a further 2 minutes, being careful not to break the smaller, delicate mushrooms.

4. Pour in 2 tablespoons of the reserved shiitake soaking liquor, the Shaoxing rice wine, soy sauce, fish sauce and oyster sauce. Leave the mushrooms to stew for 3–5 minutes, then add a sprinkling of white pepper to season.

5. Place the mushrooms in a serving dish and sprinkle over a couple of drops of sesame oil. Scatter over the shredded spring onion and chilli before serving.

PREPARATION TIME 15 MINUTES    COOKING TIME 10 MINUTES

# 64. STUNNING STIR-FRIED CHINESE MUSHROOMS

# 65. CELEBRATION SEA BASS WITH GINGER AND SPRING ONION

**SERVES 4**

**For the pickled ginger**

a 6cm piece of fresh ginger, peeled and very finely sliced

2 teaspoons rice vinegar

**For the fish**

1 x 1kg whole sea bass, gutted, scaled and cleaned

salt and ground white pepper

1 tablespoon Shaoxing rice wine or dry sherry

1 tablespoon light soy sauce

1 teaspoon sesame oil

a 3cm piece of fresh ginger, peeled and cut into matchsticks

2 spring onions, cut into matchsticks

½ a medium tomato, peeled, deseeded and diced

**For the chilli oil**

5 tablespoons groundnut oil

1 fresh red chilli, finely sliced

Feasting is super-important to the Chinese community, it's the ultimate opportunity for family and friends to join together as one and celebrate. Whether it's a baby's one-month party, a wedding or a birthday, an elaborate feast is prepared consisting of as many as twelve courses, each dish with its own special significance. The menu is run like a theatrical performance, climaxing in an all-singing, all-dancing finale. This sea bass dish will often be served as the final course. Effortlessly visual, it will arrive at the table dressed immaculately, then will be filleted right before your eyes. The perfect ending to a beautiful edible performance.

1. To make the pickled ginger, mix together the ginger and rice vinegar and leave to stand while you prepare the fish.

2. Preheat the oven to 200°C/400°F/gas 6. Line a baking tray with a sheet of tin foil, and place a sheet of baking paper over the tin foil. Place the sea bass in the centre.

3. To prepare the fish, make 3 or 4 slits along the flesh at right angles to the spine, cutting until you almost hit the bone. Season with salt and pepper. Drizzle over the Shaoxing rice wine, soy sauce and sesame oil. Scatter the ginger and spring onions over the top. Gather the foil and paper up at the edges into a package and seal well, then put the baking tray into the preheated oven and roast for 15–20 minutes, or until the fish is cooked through and flakes away easily from the bone.

4. To make the chilli oil, place the oil and chilli into a wok over a medium heat to infuse.

5. Remove the cooked fish from the oven. Carefully open the package and baste the fish with the liquid in the package. Place the fish on a serving plate.

6. Drain the pickled ginger from the vinegar, return to the bowl and add a little of the cooking juices from the fish. Stir in the tomato and season if necessary, then spoon over the fish. Pour over the hot chilli oil to serve.

PREPARATION TIME 10 MINUTES    COOKING TIME 25–30 MINUTES

**For the salmon**

1 x 1.5kg salmon, gutted
and scaled

4 tablespoons Shaoxing rice
wine or dry sherry

salt and ground white pepper

a 2cm piece of fresh
ginger, sliced

3 spring onions, trimmed
and bruised

3 cloves of garlic, peeled
and bruised

**For the sauce**

1 tablespoon groundnut oil

300g minced pork

1 tablespoon Shaoxing
rice wine or dry sherry

1–2 tablespoons light
soy sauce, to taste

1–2 teaspoons chilli bean
paste, to taste
(see page 18, optional)

300–400ml chicken or
vegetable stock, warm

3 spring onions, finely sliced
and roughly chopped

1 fresh red chilli, deseeded
and cut into matchsticks

The idea of mixing fish with meat may seem slightly odd, but think of this as Chinese surf and turf and it all makes sense. In a lot of Chinese dishes, as here, the ingredients all come together like a choir: bass, tenor, alto and soprano all joining together to create one beautiful, harmonious whole.

1. Preheat the oven to 180°C/350°F/gas 4.

2. Roll out 2 big pieces of foil and overlap them so that you have a piece big enough to wrap the whole fish in. Place the foil in a roasting tray large enough to fit the fish and rub the foil with a little oil. Slash through the skin into the flesh of the salmon at 3cm intervals along the fleshy part, at right angles to the spine.

3. Holding the fish over the roasting tray, rub it inside and out with the Shaoxing rice wine, allowing any left over to drip on to the foil. Repeat with a sprinkling of salt inside and out. Put the ginger, spring onions and garlic into the stomach cavity, then seal up the foil to enclose the fish, leaving a little room around it for air and steam to circulate.

4. Place the fish in the preheated oven and bake for 30–35 minutes, or until cooked through – the flesh should be opaque and flaky close to the bone at the thickest part. Remove from the oven and leave to rest, still in the foil, while you make the sauce.

5. Heat a wok over a high heat and add a dash of oil. When it's hot, add the minced pork and stir-fry until lightly browned. Add the Shaoxing rice wine and cook for 30 seconds. Add the soy sauce and season with a little pepper. Stir and add the chilli bean paste if using. Cook for 1–2 minutes, until fragrant.

6. Add half the warm stock and bring to a simmer. Keep simmering until the stock reduces. Taste and adjust the seasoning if necessary. Take the wok off the heat.

7. Carefully unwrap the salmon from the foil. Peel off the skin from one side of the fish and slice the salmon into pieces, 2cm thick. Arrange on a serving platter, sprinkling over the chilli pork, spring onions and fresh chilli. Serve immediately.

PREPARATION TIME 20 MINUTES    COOKING TIME 1 HOUR

# 66. BAKED SALMON WITH CHILLI PORK

'NOODLE CURE BOTH HANGOVER AND HEARTACHE'

# 7

# ONE-POT WONDERS

This chapter is full of the type of easy meals that can be rustled up without any fuss, from the most simple but nourishing noodles and broth (think healthy Pot Noodle!), to a meltingly tender braised beef short rib. I've included recipes for mussels and clams here too – quick and full of flavour, these are my Chinese one-pot wonders.

1 litre fresh chicken stock

a 4cm piece of fresh ginger,
peeled and finely chopped
into matchsticks

200g wonton noodles
(see page 23), or
thin egg noodles

2 teaspoons sesame oil

1 tablespoon oyster sauce

2 tablespoons light soy sauce

2 spring onions, finely
sliced into rounds

If this dish had arms it would wrap itself around you and give you a huge hug. Simple, clean, nourishing and delicious, at its most basic it just has three ingredients: broth, noodles and spring onions. This is A-list Pot Noodle and you will adore it. To be greeted with a steaming bowl of these noodles is to know you are loved.

1. Bring the stock to the boil. Add the fresh ginger, then reduce to a simmer and leave to cook slowly for 3–5 minutes.

2. Drop the wonton noodles into the simmering stock and cook for about 4 minutes, until just tender. Remove the noodles from the pan to two serving bowls, using a pair of tongs or a pasta fork. Drizzle with the sesame oil and mix well.

3. Add the oyster sauce and the light soy sauce to the stock and warm through to incorporate.

4. Ladle the hot broth over the noodles and sprinkle with the chopped spring onions.

PREPARATION TIME 5 MINUTES    COOKING TIME 10 MINUTES

# 67. **EASY TRADITIONAL NOODLES**

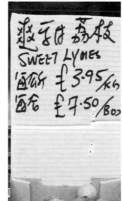

**SERVES 4**

1 x 1kg raw ham hock (not brined or salted)/pork knuckle

2 tablespoons dried lotus seeds (see page 20), rinsed

½ a cinnamon stick

2 tablespoons Shaoxing rice wine or dry sherry

½–1 tablespoon light soy sauce

½ teaspoon Chinese five-spice powder

2 heaped tablespoons goji berries (see page 20)

4 dried shiitake mushrooms, soaked in hot water for 10 minutes, drained and sliced

½ a tin of sliced lotus root (see page 21), drained

salt and ground white pepper

The moment I arrived home from school, I knew if Apor (Grandma) had come to stay. I knew this even before I saw her umbrella or shoes left at the front door, from the smell of pork and herb soup as I walked up the garden path. Apor was an amateur herbalist and knew a root, bark or bean that could cure almost anything. She was our very own Indiana Nana. This soup isn't designed to rid you of a cold or the flu, but it will stop you from catching one. A clear broth laced with goji berries, dried lotus seeds and cinnamon, engulfing a knuckle of pork, this is my culture's equivalent to Yiddish chicken soup. Often served to the sick, but more often craved by the healthy, this truly is heritage in a bowl. If you can't afford a trip to China then make this soup and you're almost there!

1. Pour 2 litres of cold water into a large saucepan. Add the ham hock and bring the water to a gentle boil. Reduce the heat and gently simmer for 2 hours, or until the meat is really tender. You may need to add extra just-boiled water from the kettle throughout the cooking time to ensure that the ham hock is always covered. Once cooked, remove the ham hock, reserving the poaching liquid, and set aside.

2. Taste the poaching liquid – if it is too strong for your taste, remove half the liquid from the pan and top up with 1 litre of water, otherwise continue with this poaching liquid as your stock for the herb soup.

3. Add the lotus seeds and cinnamon stick into the pan, along with the Shaoxing rice wine, soy sauce and Chinese five-spice powder. Stir well and bring the liquid to a gentle simmer for 20–30 minutes (or longer if you prefer a strong herb taste), until the herbs have infused their flavours into the liquid. Add the goji berries 15 minutes before the end of the cooking time.

4. Add the sliced mushrooms and lotus root and heat through. Meanwhile pull the meat off the ham hock in strips, discarding the outside skin and fat, and divide the meat equally between 4 serving bowls. Strain the soup through a sieve lined with muslin into a clean pan and reheat. Once hot, pour over the pork in the serving bowls.

PREPARATION TIME 20 MINUTES    COOKING TIME 2 HOURS 40 MINUTES

# 68. TRADITIONAL PORK, HERB AND CHINESE MUSHROOM SOUP

**SERVES 2**

50g fresh shelled peanuts,
papery inner skin removed

1 tablespoon dried shrimp,
(see page 20) soaked in hot
water for 15 minutes

½ a fresh red chilli,
finely chopped

a 1.5cm piece of fresh ginger,
grated or very finely chopped

2 spring onions, shredded

1 clove of garlic,
crushed or grated

200g vermicelli noodles,
soaked and drained according
to packet instructions
(see page 22)

1 teaspoon fish sauce

1–2 teaspoons light
soy sauce, to taste

a handful of fresh coriander,
roughly chopped

As much as I adore glamorous and flamboyant food, my palate is split like Dr Jekyll and Mr Hyde. When I'm dining with friends, I love the big performance of a stylized meal, but when I'm home alone after a hard day's work, sometimes I crave the most simple and honest of foods. Glass noodle salad is not only quick and easy to prepare, it's also quick and easy to devour, packed full of flavour and with the hidden surprise of the boiled peanuts. I challenge even the most pretentious of diners not to fall in love with this simple dish.

1. Bring a pan of water to the boil, then add the peanuts and boil them for 10–15 minutes, or until softened slightly. Drain, then dry on kitchen paper. Once dry, crush the peanuts or chop them into small pieces and put them in a bowl, retaining a few whole peanuts to dress the salad.

2. Chop the drained dried shrimp roughly and add to the bowl along with the chilli, ginger, spring onions and garlic. Mix well, bashing the ingredients in the bowl with a wooden spoon to break them up slightly as you mix. Add the vermicelli noodles and mix well with the other ingredients. Season with the fish sauce and soy sauce, combining everything together well.

3. Finish the noodles with a handful of coriander, mixing it in roughly, and serve.

PREPARATION TIME 10 MINUTES    COOKING TIME 15 MINUTES

# 69. GLASS NOODLE WARM SALAD WITH PEANUTS AND DRIED SHRIMP

500ml chicken stock

6–10 dried red dates
(see page 20), or
2 tablespoons goji
berries (see page 20)

2 tablespoons red bean curd
(see page 20)

2 tablespoons groundnut oil

2 cloves of garlic,
peeled and crushed

a 2–3cm piece of fresh
ginger, thinly sliced

6–8 spring onions, crushed

4 x skinless chicken breasts
(approx. 500g), sliced

100ml Shaoxing rice wine,
sweet sherry or brandy

salt and ground white pepper

It seems that every country and culture around the world boasts some kind of restorative chicken soup, and the Chinese are no different. This is my dad's version and it has been comforting my family for years. The red berries included in this dish not only resemble small glistening jewels but are so uniquely flavoured that they infuse the broth with a herbal, almost medicinal, aroma. You are sure to find red dates or goji berries in one of the many Chinese herbal shops that seem to be adorning high streets up and down the country.

1. Heat the chicken stock in a large pan and add the red dates and red bean curd. Bring to the boil, then reduce the heat and simmer for 30–40 minutes. Drain and discard the flavourings, topping up the stock to 400ml with water if it has over-reduced.

2. Heat your wok over a medium to high heat and add a glug of oil. When it's hot, add the garlic, ginger and spring onions, then add the chicken slices and fry for 2–3 minutes.

3. Turn the heat down, pour in the Shaoxing rice wine and gently cook for a further 2–3 minutes.

4. Add the contents of the wok to the pan of stock and simmer together for a further 8–10 minutes. Season with salt and pepper, and serve.

PREPARATION TIME 10 MINUTES    COOKING TIME 50 MINUTES

# 70. DAD'S DRUNKEN CHICKEN

**SERVES 4**

2 tablespoons groundnut oil

2 cloves of garlic, peeled and finely sliced

2 sticks of celery, finely sliced at an angle

3 spring onions, finely sliced into rounds

1.5kg fresh mussels, scrubbed and de-bearded

75ml Shaoxing rice wine or dry sherry

2 tablespoons black beans, soaked in water for 10 minutes and drained

2 tablespoons oyster sauce

1 tablespoon dark soy sauce

There's something absolutely amazing about serving something in its original packaging, whether that's a fresh lobster in its coral-coloured casing, Grandma's eggs in their cracked-and-dipped soy sauce shells or the mother of all showy shellfish, the beautiful mussel. Mussels are naturally very sweet and have a wonderful texture – in one mouthful you can be guaranteed soft flesh contrasting with a meaty bite. Here, the sweetness of the fish works in perfect harmony with the bitterness of the black beans. Finished result . . . food nirvana.

1. Heat the groundnut oil in a wok or saucepan with a tight-fitting lid over a medium to high heat. When hot, add the garlic, celery and spring onions. Stir-fry these vegetables for 1–2 minutes until they are soft and beginning to colour.

2. Increase the heat to maximum and add the mussels, stirring so they are coated with the rest of the ingredients. Once they are combined, pour in the Shaoxing rice wine and immediately cover the wok with a lid.

3. Leave the mussels to cook for 4–5 minutes. Mussels are cooked when they have opened to reveal the coral-coloured flesh on the inside. Do not eat any that remain closed. As soon as the mussels are opened, tip the entire contents of the wok into a sieve set over a bowl, shaking the mixture to make sure all the liquid has drained through.

4. Place the wok back on the heat over a low flame, then pour the sieved liquid back into the wok and bring to the boil. Once it's bubbling, add the black beans, oyster and soy sauce. Cook for 4–5 minutes to reduce the mixture by a quarter.

5. Put the mussels back in the wok, along with all the other ingredients gathered in the sieve. Heat through and serve immediately.

PREPARATION TIME 10 MINUTES    COOKING TIME 15 MINUTES

# 71. MUSSELS WITH BLACK BEAN SAUCE

2 tablespoons groundnut oil

3 sticks of celery, cut diagonally in 1cm-thick slices

1–2 tablespoons curry powder

1.25kg fresh clams, thoroughly washed to remove all grit, covered in cold water for 20 minutes

100ml Shaoxing rice wine or dry sherry

Speed-eating is a skill taught to Chinese children from a very young age – especially if you grew up in the Family Wan, who are fast and furious! Mealtimes are comparable to ancient Kung Fu schools where disciples and sifu masters go head-to-head in a quest for 'saving face' and tummy victory. The contest begins as soon as the first plate of delicious food is dropped into the ring – no warning bell is rung, it's simply a case of do or die! Within moments, a flurry of sleeves are pushed up arms, chopsticks swiped from the table and bowls scooped into hands; before you know it, battle has begun. The combatants leap into action, barely making eye contact, hands darting across the table with skill and precision. Shiitake mushrooms are flipped and caught, clams spun and grappled, water chestnuts wrestled and intercepted . . . Chopstick martial arts: 'Sifu master . . . I obey, but now I have learnt!'

1. Heat the oil in a wok or saucepan with a tight-fitting lid over a medium to high heat. Once the oil is hot, add the celery. Stir-fry the celery for 2 minutes until it begins to soften.

2. Add the curry powder and fry with the celery for 30 seconds, stirring frequently to avoid burning. Mix in the clams before pouring in the Shaoxing rice wine, then place a lid on top.

3. Steam the clams for 4–5 minutes. They are cooked when they open. Do not eat any that remain closed.

4. Arrange the clams in a bowl and serve as part of a larger meal.

PREPARATION TIME 20 MINUTES    COOKING TIME 15 MINUTES

**SERVES 4**

3 tablespoons groundnut oil

4 short ribs of beef

2 star anise

a 4cm piece of orange peel

a 5cm piece of fresh ginger,
peeled and sliced

3 cloves of garlic, peeled
and bruised

100ml Shaoxing rice wine
or dry sherry

250ml light soy sauce

250ml water

2 tablespoons toasted
sesame seeds

This cut of meat is criminally underused in the West. Cheap and full of flavour, enhanced by the complex background flavours of anise and orange, the humble beef rib will not disappoint. So meltingly tender, I know this will soon become a regular dish you use to wow dinner guests.

1. Pre-heat your oven to 170°C/325°F/gas 3.

2. Heat the oil in a large oven-proof saucepan with a lid over a high heat. When hot, add the beef ribs in a single layer and brown on all sides. If your pot is not big enough then fry the meat in batches.

3. Once all the ribs are browned, reduce the heat to medium and add the star anise, orange peel, ginger and garlic. Stir-fry for 2 minutes.

4. Pour in the Shaoxing rice wine, soy sauce and water and bring to the boil. Once it is boiling place the lid on top and put the saucepan in the oven to cook for 1 hour.

5. Take the saucepan out of the oven and remove the lid. Increase the temperature of the oven to 200°C/400°F/gas 6, and, once it has heated up, place the saucepan back in the oven and cook for a further 30 minutes. By this time the ribs should be meltingly tender and the sauce reduced.

6. Sprinkle the ribs with toasted sesame seeds and serve with congee (see page 80) or steamed rice and pak choi.

PREPARATION TIME 10 MINUTES    COOKING TIME 2 HOURS

# 73. **BRAISED BEEF SHORT RIB**

3 tablespoons groundnut oil

150g minced pork

2 anchovy fillets, drained and finely sliced

4 cloves of garlic, peeled and finely sliced

2 aubergines, trimmed and chopped into 3cm dice

2 tablespoons light soy sauce

1 tablespoon dark soy sauce

200ml water

3 teaspoons sesame oil

2 spring onions, sliced

Two really popular ingredients in Chinese food are aubergines and pork . . . no surprise then that this dish is a traditional favourite. It also has a surprise ingredient that's unexpected but just works: anchovies. Hidden beneath the hemline of the pork and aubergines is salty fish sauce; the anchovies add a new layer for your tastebuds to explore and adore. Full of flavour and distinctiveness, this meal will wow the crowds and leave everybody wanting more. Nothing wrong with a little food cabaret at the table!

1. Heat the oil in a wok over a high heat. When hot, add the minced pork and stir-fry for 2 minutes until the pork starts to brown at the edges.

2. Add the anchovy fillets and garlic and stir-fry for another 2 minutes. Add the cubed aubergines and stir intermittently for the next 3–4 minutes, until the aubergines begin to brown and soften at the edges.

3. Reduce the heat to medium, pour in both types of soy sauce and add half the water. Bring to the boil and put a lid on the wok. Simmer the mixture for about 20 minutes. It's important to ensure the pan does not run dry, so keep checking and add more water, using the entire 200ml if necessary.

4. Cook the aubergines down until they are virtually falling apart. At this point, stir in the sesame oil and remove to a plate. Sprinkle liberally with sliced spring onions and serve with rice.

PREPARATION TIME 10 MINUTES    COOKING TIME 30 MINUTES

# 74. BRAISED AUBERGINE WITH PORK

**SERVES 3–4**

1 tablespoon groundnut oil

250g runner beans, cut at an
angle into 2cm diamonds

4 fresh red chillies,
split lengthways

75g minced pork

1–2 teaspoons Shaoxing
rice wine or dry sherry

1–2 teaspoons light soy sauce,
to taste

1 tablespoon preserved
mustard greens, shredded
(see page 22, optional)

salt and ground white pepper

1 tablespoon sesame oil,
to serve

Sometimes it seems different cultures can share the most unlikely of ingredients. In this case I'm talking about runner beans; so quintessentially British, yet so commonly used in the Sichuan region of China. Of course, because this is a Sichuan dish, expect fire and flavour.

1. Heat a wok over a high heat. Add a dash of oil and stir-fry the beans and chillies for 4 minutes until blistered on the outside (not burnt) and tender in the middle. Remove from the wok and leave to one side.

2. Heat another dash of oil in the pan. Add the minced pork and fry over a high heat, for between 30 seconds and 1 minute, or until cooked through, adding the Shaoxing rice wine and soy sauce to taste. Add the cooked beans and chillies, and stir to combine.

3. Taste and adjust the seasoning as necessary. Finish with a little drizzle of sesame oil and serve immediately.

PREPARATION TIME 5 MINUTES    COOKING TIME 7 MINUTES

# 75. SICHUAN DRY-FRIED BEANS

'TO PLEASE ALL AT THE TABLE MAKE PLENTY'

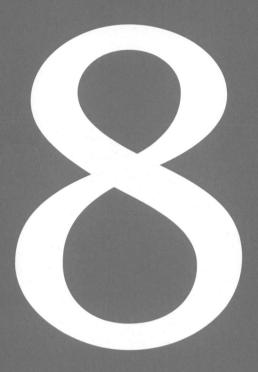

# 8

# MODERN DISHES

I've called this chapter modern dishes, as it includes recipes with a slight twist to the traditional way of making them, like salt and pepper pork chops or, if you love fish as I do, grilled mackerel with sesame spinach and steamed cod with greens. These are dishes that I absolutely love to eat. Quick, delicious, healthy – all the boxes are ticked!

800g baby squid (calamari),
left whole

I tablespoon groundnut oil

I teaspoon shrimp paste
(see page 22)

a 3cm piece of fresh ginger,
peeled and cut into
matchsticks

2 spring onions, trimmed
and finely sliced

Chinese cuisine is visual but also full of sound. My dad says that Chinese food isn't for living, it's a way of life. You want it to become a performance, for it to stimulate all your senses. Dad does two types of cooking – the dramatic, Royal Shakespeare-type performance, or simple, quick and functional. One of his best homestyle dishes, I think, is celery simply covered in butter and grilled, served with dried squid. It sounds a bit disgusting, but it tastes unbelievable and it would go perfectly with these skewers of grilled fresh squid as an alternative to the pickled cucumbers.

1. Wash the baby squid, then set them aside and let them drip dry.

2. Cut wooden skewers to the length that will fit your griddle pan comfortably and then soak the skewers in warm water for 10 minutes.

3. Heat a small frying pan over a medium heat. When it's hot, drizzle in the oil and mash in the shrimp paste, to dissolve it a little. Mix in the ginger and spring onions, remove from the heat and leave to cool for 2 minutes.

4. Place the squid into a bowl and add the flavourings from the frying pan, mix really well into the squid using your hands. Spear the squid on to the skewers, smothering the paste all over the squid. Preheat the griddle until very hot and then cook the squid (in batches, if necessary) for 2–3 minutes, turning often to blacken the outsides slightly.

5. Serve straight away with a pickled vegetable salad or pickled cucumber (see page 98).

PREPARATION TIME 10 MINUTES    COOKING TIME 8 MINUTES

# 76. **GRILLED BABY SQUID**

**SERVES 2–4**

1 x 650g piece of thick pork belly, bones removed

1 tablespoon rice vinegar

juice of 1 lemon

1 heaped teaspoon Chinese five-spice powder

1 teaspoon ground white pepper

2 teaspoons salt

This dish is classic Poppa Wan. When he makes it he hangs the pork to cook over a tray in his oven, but you can place the meat on the top shelf of the oven with a tray underneath to catch the juices to get the same result. I've served it with pickled mushrooms here (see page 222), but the traditional accompaniment is simply a bowl of sugar to dip the meat into. It's that sweet and savoury vibe again.

1. Clean the skin of the pork by scraping it with a sharp knife, then prick the skin all over with a fork. Turn the pork over so that it is meat side up, and score it with a knife in lines about 5cm apart, cutting through about half the thickness of the meat. Rub the skin with vinegar and lemon juice, and rub the meat side with five-spice powder, pepper and half the salt.

2. Now turn the pork so that it is skin side up again and rub it with the remaining salt. Place the meat on a wire rack over a tray and leave it uncovered in your fridge overnight.

3. Take the pork out of the fridge 2 hours before cooking so that it can warm up to room temperature.

4. Preheat the oven to 170°C/325°F/gas 3. Place the pork, still on its wire rack, on the top shelf of the oven, with a tray underneath. Roast for 40 minutes, then turn the oven up to 220°C/425°F/gas 7 and continue roasting for another 20 minutes. Keep checking the pork to make sure it is cooking evenly.

5. When the pork is cooked, remove it from the oven and leave it to cool for 20 minutes before slicing and serving.

PREPARATION TIME 10–12 HOURS    COOKING TIME 1 HOUR

# 77. **ROASTED CRISPY PORK BELLY**

# 78. PICKLED MUSHROOMS

**SERVES 4–6 AS A SIDE DISH**

1 tablespoon groundnut oil

8 fresh shiitake
mushrooms, sliced

300g assorted fresh mushrooms
(such as chestnut, enoki and
oyster), cleaned and sliced
or separated

2–3 teaspoons caster sugar

½ tablespoon light soy sauce

3 tablespoons Chinkiang black
rice vinegar (see page 20)

salt and ground white pepper

1 whole fresh red chilli, split
lengthways

a 3cm piece of
fresh ginger, sliced

I dream of a day when these delicious grenades of sour, savoury flavour are laid on tables next to pickled onions and traditional roast ham. They are a perfect accompaniment to most savoury food from both East and West.

1. Heat a wok over a medium heat. Add a dash of oil and heat, then add the shiitake mushrooms. Cook for 2–3 minutes over a medium heat then add the rest of the mushrooms and continue to cook for 1 more minute.

2. Add the sugar, soy sauce and rice vinegar and cook for 30 seconds, or until the sugar has dissolved. Remove the wok from the heat and add the chilli and ginger. Taste, and season with a pinch of salt and pepper if necessary. Remove everything from the wok and leave to cool. Transfer to an airtight container and leave to pickle overnight.

3. Before serving the mushrooms as part of a Chinese meal, remove and discard the chilli and ginger slices, and drain the liquid off.

PREPARATION TIME 10 MINUTES    MARINATING TIME OVERNIGHT

**For the clams**

6 fresh razor clams

a 2cm piece of fresh ginger,
peeled and finely chopped

1 spring onion, trimmed and
finely chopped

½ teaspoon light soy sauce

**For the garlic and
chilli sprinkles**

groundnut oil

1 fresh red chilli,
deseeded and finely sliced

3 cloves of garlic, peeled
and finely sliced

The fried and dried sprinkles of chilli and garlic in this dish can lend their magic to most savoury dishes. From popcorn to plain rice, they work it like all good accessories do, accentuating all that they dress. For this recipe I have chosen to sprinkle their magic over steamed razor clams. Delicious!

1. To make the garlic and chilli sprinkles, heat a 2cm deep layer of oil in a pan or wok. Once hot, add the chilli and fry for 10 seconds, then add the garlic and continue to fry until golden and crisp. Remove as soon as the garlic turns dark golden. Place in a single layer on kitchen paper and leave to dry out, placing more kitchen paper on top to absorb any oil.

2. Meanwhile, set a bamboo steamer large enough to hold 6 open razor clams over a wok of boiling water. Place the clams on a heatproof plate that will fit the steamer. Put the plate into the steamer and steam for 30 seconds, at which point the clams should open slightly.

3. Once the clams are open, sprinkle some of the ginger and spring onion into each of them. Add a drop of soy sauce to each clam, then replace the steamer lid and continue to steam for a further 2 minutes, or until the clams have opened fully and are cooked through.

4. Remove the clams from the steamer and serve immediately, with the garlic and chilli sprinkles scattered over them.

PREPARATION TIME 10 MINUTES      COOKING TIME 5 MINUTES

# 79. STEAMED RAZOR CLAMS WITH GARLIC AND CHILLI SPRINKLES

4 mackerel fillets, cleaned
and pin-boned

salt

500g mature spinach,
thoroughly washed and
with the root removed

1 clove of garlic, peeled
and finely grated

1–2 tablespoons light
soy sauce

2 teaspoons toasted
sesame oil

1 teaspoon sesame seeds

With omega-3 fatty acids from the fish, iron from the spinach and magnesium and calcium from the sesame seeds, you'll find that this dish gives you a health kick like no other. Deliciously virtuous.

1. Preheat your grill to about two thirds of the maximum temperature.

2. Season the mackerel fillets generously with salt. Place on a tray, skin side up, and slide under the grill reasonably close to the element. Grill the mackerel for about 8 minutes. There should be no need to turn the fish halfway through. You are aiming for the skin to become crisp and blistered in places.

3. Meanwhile, heat a large pan of water. Once the water has reached a rolling boil, add the spinach. Cook the spinach for about a minute. As soon as it is ready, drain the spinach in a colander and cool immediately under cold running water.

4. Once the spinach has been thoroughly cooled, squeeze it with your hands to drain as much of the excess water as possible. Place the cooled spinach in a bowl and add the garlic, soy sauce and sesame oil. Mix together well. Sprinkle over the sesame seeds.

5. Serve the mackerel and spinach as a light lunch, or double up the amounts and serve with rice as a more substantial dinner.

PREPARATION TIME 10 MINUTES    COOKING TIME 8 MINUTES

# 80. SIMPLE GRILLED MACKEREL WITH SESAME SPINACH

**SERVES 2**

groundnut oil, to shallow fry

3 tablespoons plain flour

3 tablespoons cornflour

1 teaspoon salt

1 teaspoon ground
white pepper

2 fresh red chillies,
split lengthways

4 spring onions, sliced
lengthways and then in half to
make 4 long pieces

4 cloves of garlic, peeled
and left whole

2 pork chops

Sometimes you deserve a little of what you fancy. When that time comes, look no further than this dish. A little naughty, but well worth the calories. Eat it with a green salad to realign your dietary karma!

1. Heat the oil in a wok or high-sided frying pan. You are aiming for a temperature of about 160°C/325°F. If you don't have a heatproof thermometer, the oil is at the right temperature when a cube of bread takes 30 seconds to brown in the oil.

2. Mix together the flours, salt and pepper, then toss the prepared vegetables in the mixture.

3. Shake off any excess flour from the vegetables before carefully placing them in the oil to fry, then shallow fry for about 3 minutes. The vegetables are ready when they are just beginning to brown. Remove the cooked vegetables from the wok and place them on kitchen roll to drain the excess oil.

4. Pat the pork chops dry with a piece of kitchen roll before tossing them in the flour mix. Shake off the excess flour and place them carefully in the hot oil. Shallow fry the chops on each side for 3–5 minutes, although cooking times will vary according to the thickness of the chops. They should be ready when they've taken on a lovely even brown colour.

5. Remove the pork chops from the wok and place them on some kitchen roll to absorb any excess oil. Leave to rest for 2 minutes.

6. Top the pork chops with the mixed, fried vegetables and serve with pickled cucumber and salad as a light lunch, or add rice for a more substantial dinner.

PREPARATION TIME 10 MINUTES    COOKING TIME 12 MINUTES

# 81. **SALT AND PEPPER PORK CHOPS**

**SERVES 4**

4 x 175g cod fillets, skin on
and bones removed
or pinboned

300g tenderstem broccoli

4 tablespoons light soy sauce

2 tablespoons Shaoxing rice
wine or dry sherry

a 4cm piece of fresh ginger,
peeled and finely cut
into matchsticks

3 spring onions, finely sliced
into rounds

3 tablespoons sesame oil

A complete meal for family and friends on one plate. Start it cooking, and by the time you've finished applying your lipgloss it'll be ready to gobble down.

1. Place the cod fillets and broccoli on a high-sided plate that will fit in your steamer. Do not pile ingredients on top of each other; use a second steamer if necessary. Scatter over the spring onions. Combine the soy sauce, Shaoxing rice wine and sesame oil and spoon over the fish and broccoli before sprinkling the ginger on top.

2. Place the plate in a steamer basket and cook over boiling water for 10 minutes, or until the fish has just turned from opaque to white and the broccoli has started to soften.

3. Once it is cool enough to handle, remove the plate from the steamer and serve with bowls of rice.

PREPARATION TIME 10 MINUTES    COOKING TIME 10–15 MINUTES

# 82. **STEAMED COD WITH TENDERSTEM BROCCOLI**

# INDEX

Page references in **bold** indicate photographs

## ACKNOWLEDGEMENTS

I would like to thank the following for all their hard work and dedication in helping to make this journey happen:

From Optomen Television: Pat, Paul, Emily, Karen, Tom, Colin, Rob, Pooch, Sarah, Lianne, Greg, Rob, Leonie, Richard, Conor, Robbie, Emma, Rae, Ian and Joe

From Penguin Books: Lindsey, John, Louise, Sarah, Nick, Debbie, Tamsin, Emma, Hannah, Juliette, Katya and Liz

For the photography: Jemma, and her assistant Lisa

From my personal team and my good friends: Carol, Mark, Elise, Charlie, Carrie, Sue, Stephen, Naoko and E'lain.

And to my family: Oilen, Kwoklyn, Mum and Dad . . . And, of course, the three wise men!